StatelyLiving

The changing face of historic houses

Published by VisitBritain Publishing in association with the Historic Houses Association

VisitBritain Publishing
Thames Tower, Blacks Road, London W6 9EL

First published 2007

ISBN 978-0-7095-8403-2
Product code: TNSTLIV

A CIP catalogue record for this book is available from the British Library.

The information contained in this publication has been published in good faith on the basis of information submitted to VisitBritain and is believed to be correct at time of going to press. Nevertheless, VisitBritain regrets that it cannot guarantee complete accuracy and all liability for loss, disappointment, negligence or other damages caused by reliance on the information contained in this publication, is hereby excluded.

Designed and produced for VisitBritain Publishing by Susanna Geoghegan Gift Publishing Consultancy
Printed in China

Contents

Foreword

Stately Living forms part of the 'Then and Now' series which has been published in association with the Historic Houses Association (HHA).

As its title suggests, the series looks at the life and work of Britain's historic houses today – attracting, as they do, more than 15 million visitors a year, providing employment for upwards of 10,000 people (who annually earn in excess of £85 million) and contributing an estimated £1.6– £2 billion each year to the rural economy – and compares and contrasts this with times past, when these houses and their estates were largely the exclusive preserve of their owners and their guests.

It is a fascinating and inspiring subject, which has been made all the more illuminating thanks to the very considerable help of a large number of people: owners who have set aside time in busy schedules to give interviews and answer questions, administrators who have coordinated research, archivists who have made available much valuable material from past and present, members of staff who have broken off what they were doing to chat freely about their work (which in a number of cases spans several decades at the same property).

We extend our very grateful thanks to them all, in particular the following, who have been closely involved with the series throughout its evolution:

At the HHA itself, Peter Sinclair and Fiona Attenborough.

At Ballindalloch Castle, Mrs Clare Macpherson-Grant Russell Laird of Ballindalloch, her husband Oliver Russell and Fenella Corr.

At Chatsworth, the Duke of Devonshire, Simon Seligman, Charles Noble, Stuart Band, Andrew Peppitt, Diana Naylor and Glyn Motley.

At Eastnor Castle, James Hervey-Bathurst and Simon Foster.

At Fonmon Castle, Sir Brooke Boothby.

At Loseley Park, Michael More-Molyneux, Major James More-Molyneux, Nichola Cheriton-Sutton and Isabel Sullivan (who looks after the Loseley archives at Surrey History Centre).

At Newby Hall, Richard Compton, Robin Compton and Stuart Gill.

At Powderham Castle, the Earl and Countess of Devon, Lady Katherine Watney, Clare Crawshaw, Felicity Harper, Ginny Bowman and Christine Manning.

At Ripley Castle, Sir Thomas Ingilby and Alison Crawford.

In addition we would like to thank three of the above as authors who have kindly permitted us to quote from their work. They, and their books, are: Sir Thomas Ingilby, *Yorkshire's Great Houses* (Dalesman Publishing 2005); James More-Molyneux, *The Loseley Challenge* (Hodder & Stoughton 1995); Clare Macpherson-Grant Russell, *"I Love Food"* (Heritage House Group Ltd 2006).

Introduction

The conservation and survival of today's historic houses depends in large measure on the ingenuity and enterprise of their owners. Forty years ago the sixth Marquess of Bath attracted worldwide publicity when he opened the Lions of Longleat Safari Park. Twenty-seven years earlier he had been heavily criticised when he made Longleat the first house in the country to be opened on a regular commercial basis. Entrance cost 2s 6d (12.5p), the night watchman's wife ran a small café in the basement and the family helped with car parking. Much has changed in the last sixty years and many have seen the wisdom of following Lord Bath's entrepreneurial example.

Stately Living makes use of personal anecdotes and archive material to illustrate the enormous changes which historic houses and the lives of their owners have undergone. From the dowager owner of one ancient home who, after washing her hair, had to time moving across a corridor from one part of her flat to another in order to avoid startling a tour group of visitors with her dripping locks, to the lady of another equally venerable castle, who had to shuffle down a stone stairway on her backside to lead a petrified visitor to the bottom and safety, this book looks at the challenges present-day owners have had to rise to compared with the more detached existence of their forebears.

From Tithes
to Tourism

'At the time when England decided to enter the Great War many foresaw that whatever might be the result of the struggle, great social changes would be bound to result. For the first time a large part of the population hitherto closely connected with the soil were about to be brought into contact with the outside world, in consequence of which new ideas would be imported into country villages inhabited by people who had for generations been content to live in a quiet unprogressive way. To some extent these anticipations turned out correct, a very perceptible change having taken place in the mentality of the proletariat after the great struggle had ended. The war, however, had other more unexpected results as regards another class which even before the outbreak of hostilities had found it difficult to make both ends meet – landowners and squires having for some years found themselves confronted with taxation, likely to drive them out of their ancient homes. No wonder then that the largely increased amount demanded as a result of the war has led to many

A seemingly timeless reflection of late Victorian country house life soon to be lost in the decline that followed the First World War.

11

ancestral homes being left empty or put to other uses than those for which they were built.'

So wrote Ralph Nevill at the beginning of his book *English Country House Life* which was published in 1925 – eleven years after the First World War had started, seven years after it had finished and twenty years before the end of the Second World War would mark another significant change in the life and work of Britain's historic houses.

Much of what he predicted came about. Many fine houses fell into disrepair and had to be demolished in the end. Just as distressing was the disappearance of lovingly maintained gardens and grounds that had reached their heyday in the generation that preceded the outbreak of Nevill's 'Great War'. Other fine houses were converted to serve a variety of new functions from sanatoria to schools. Everywhere families, whose livelihood had for generations been tied to the land, found their traditional incomes slumping and the way of life on which their ancient homes had been sustained for centuries eroding faster than ever in their history.

This cycle of decline and decay was not inexorable or inevitable, however. Three quarters of a century after Nevill's book was published many historic houses are busier than they have ever been. Many now employ more people than they have ever done before and many are achieving a level of financial stability and sustainability that they have not known for a century.

Great changes may have taken place in the world around them, but these houses and the two generations of owners who have been their custodians since the middle of the twentieth century have responded with significant changes of their own. State rooms and stately gardens that were once the exclusive preserve of the owners and their guests, now entertain tens of thousands of visitors every year: some to spend a few hours as part of a day out; others joining in wedding celebrations or attending corporate hospitality events. Owners and their families have condensed their own accommodation into a flat ('a four-bedroom semi', as the son of one current owner described their family's quarters), leaving the rest of their houses free to be utilised by the catering

Like Tortworth Court on the previous page, many houses and sublime gardens were 'lost' in the aftermath of the First World War when many family fortunes and staffing levels were radically reduced and country house life changed irrevocably.

Powderham Castle and its gardens as they appeared in the mid-eighteenth century.

and hospitality businesses they are building, and on which the maintenance and survival of their ancestral homes increasingly depends.

The Earl of Devon, who runs the Powderham Castle estate near Exeter, where his family have been living for over 600 years, gives a contemporary view of the changes in estate income that have taken place and been put in place. 'The popular view of an English country estate,' he writes in the guide to Powderham Castle, 'is of a large historic mansion surrounded by numerous tenant farms whose rents pay for the upkeep of the large house. There may have been past times when this was reality, but it is certainly not the case today. A modern estate, such as Powderham, is every bit a business and needs to adjust and develop with the times to be competitive, economically viable and to remain afloat in the ever-changing seas of fiscal and political policy.'

It is a testament to the affection for and wholehearted commitment to their homes shown by post-war owners of historic houses that sizeable changes have taken place without significantly altering the appeal and attraction of what they have struggled to preserve: the houses themselves, their gardens and parklands, and the wider estates with their range of housing and traditional agricultural buildings, woodlands, pastures and arable land. To gain some understanding of the contrasts in estate incomes 'then' and 'now', we need first to get a glimpse of the financial climate in which owners of great houses in past centuries lived and worked.

Here is Ralph Nevill again, describing the golden era of Britain's great landed estates: 'A typical instance of an old English country house was Compton Verney, so well described by the late Lord Willoughby de Broke in the volume of recollections published after his death. During the halcyon days of the nineteenth century this mansion had its own brew-house as well as chapel, while a ton of coal a day was burnt in the kitchen, where a glorious sirloin hung by a chain turning slowly round during the process of basting; meanwhile, Compton Verney rejoiced in a

household of contented retainers and the owner drew an ample rent-roll from a substantial tenantry. That was the age of high prices, stout broadcloth, top boots and old port, while country house life as a rule was as orderly as the well-kept parks and as dignified as the ancient oaks which adorned them. Income tax and death duties then practically did not exist. This golden era for country gentlemen lasted on till about 1880, when agricultural depression began to press upon owners of land. Up to the end of the last century, five thousand a year went a great way; while the squirearchy, then more or less supreme, hunted

and shot to their hearts' content without any disquieting shocks in the way of Radical legislation.'

Such 'halcyon days' came about in part thanks to shrewd and careful financial planning that enhanced the fortunes of many estates. The second Marquess of Bath hit on the idea of persuading his tenant farmers to pay twenty years' rent in advance, which presented him with a capital sum large enough to renovate the interior of Longleat and add a number of offices. In less than thirty years, between 1749 and 1778, the first Duke of Northumberland reorganised property around his home at Alnwick so profitably that the annual rent income increased from £8,607 to £50,000.

Agriculture was not the only economic sector through which estate fortunes were augmented. In the mid-1920s a writer in the *Quarterly Review* commented on the important part that the investment of estate profits played in the growth of manufacturing industry. 'Of late years,' he began, 'no one seems to remember, or realize that but for the landlord and the yeoman, modern industrial England would never have come into being. Utterly fallacious indeed is the idea entertained by urban workers that the interests of those living by the land are not worthy of attention. Had it not been for the latter, the great cities with their commerce and manufactories would never have reached their present development. The wealthy landowners of the past made large sums of money from well-ordered estates, and were consequently enabled to invest such profits in industrial enterprise. During the middle portion of the nineteenth century, the latter was in some respects of real assistance to agriculture. Railways, for instance, which now irritate the farmer by high charges and none too efficient services, then afforded very adequate transport facilities, and thus indirectly maintained the prosperity of country families, while the squires were able to spend money on farm implements and farms, improve stock and repair and re-erect houses. There was then a national feeling of confidence in agriculture. In 1854 four million acres still grew corn. Various events, such as the Crimean War and the contest in America between North and South, did no harm to English trade. In the last thirty years of the nineteenth century, however, England and Wales lost two million of the acres devoted to corn, while farmers also suffered severely from the beginning of the importing of frozen meat. The demand for cheap food had by this time become so insistent that, a return to Protection being seemingly out of the question, landlords allowed large areas of tilled soil to be laid down to grass, while considerable tracts of once fertile ground became desolate and neglected.'

Mining was another source of huge economic growth for nineteenth-century investors. The Duchess of Cleveland developed her home at Battle into a noted centre of aristocratic hospitality among Sussex country houses; the Battle gardens in particular received lavish attention. None of this would have been possible, however, were it not for the income accruing from her other estate at Raby in Country Durham. The colliery income from the area where the Duke and Duchess took their title was enormous. When the first Duke of Cleveland died in 1842, he was worth £110,000 a year, and had amounting to £1,000,000 in cash on deposit in the bank. Although his eldest son only inherited the entailed income, that still assured him an annual income of £70,000, while two other sons were left equally well off.

At much the same time another aristocratic lady was playing her part in the growth of Victorian industry. Following the death of her husband, Lady Londonderry found a flair for business and threw herself into coal mining, eventually employing 4,000 miners in her collieries. Benjamin Disraeli went to stay with her at Seaham Hall in 1861 and recorded afterwards, 'This is a remarkable place and our hostess a remarkable woman. Twenty miles hence she has a palace (Wynard) in a vast park, with forest rides and antlered deer, and all the splendid accessories of feudal life. But she prefers living in a hall on the shores of the German Ocean, surrounded by her collieries and her blast furnaces and her railroads, and the unceasing telegraphs, with a port hewn out of solid rock, screw-steamers and four thousand pitmen under her control. In the town of Seaham Harbour, a mile off, she has a regular office, a fine stone building with her name and

arms in front, and her flag flying above; and here she transacts, with innumerable agents, immense business and I remember her twenty-five years ago a mere fine lady; nay, the finest in London! But one must find excitement if one has brains.'

In a great many cases, though, aristocratic brains sought 'excitement' in areas of public life other than industry and commerce. As Ralph Nevill puts it, 'A good family library indeed was considered an indispensable adjunct of a country house, and many a country gentleman who cut a good figure at Westminster owed his culture and learning to the well-bound books amongst which he had been taught as a child to browse …

'But from these temples of learning came no business men, the manipulation of other people's money in order to benefit one's own pocket not being then considered a suitable profession for the son of a country gentleman …

'The most popular professions with the aristocracy and gentry were the army and navy, the feeling which produced such a state of affairs being akin to that concerning the *noblesse*

A group of Oxford University students destined for service in the army.

de l'épée which prevailed in pre-Revolutionary France …

'It is said that the duration of a country family in England used to be about three generations, a state of affairs not difficult to realize when one remembers that the accepted mode of training an heir to large possessions was to send him to some fast college at Oxford or Cambridge, or into a crack regiment where he learnt to go the pace. For a youth who was to inherit large possessions a military career of this sort nine times out of ten entailed great extravagance, whilst his almost continual presence in London brought him in contact with a number of pleasures and allurements which tended to make him frivolous and unthinking. What could such a man know of the needs of his tenantry, or how to manage an estate?'

This sense of detachment from the income-producing activities on which great estates depended left many families ill-prepared for the series of financial shocks that began to impact on their fortunes with the agricultural recession that clouded much of Queen Victoria's reign. By the middle of the nineteenth century many stately homes were facing financial difficulties. Commenting on this, Richard Monckton-Milnes, politician, philanthropist and great social reformer, wrote in 1845, 'The gradual pauperization of the upper classes is distinct and tangible. I never saw so many houses to let. Barouches turned into flies, chariots into broughams. There are fewer balls and it is getting rather respectable than not to have little money to spend.'

Declines in traditional income were compounded by increases in taxation. Following the revisions to death duty in Sir William Harcourt's 1894 budget, which introduced Estate Duty, many families took steps to safeguard their inheritance. As Lady Paget noted, 'Lady Salisbury told me that Lord Salisbury had made over Hatfield and everything else to Lord Cranbourne on account of the fearful death duties. Also that Lord Eustace Cecil had made himself and family into a joint stock company and that Lord Selbourne had made everything over to his son. In the meantime all the works of art are going to America and to Russia.'

Others looked to alternative ways of refreshing their finances. Within ten years of Sir William Harcourt's reforms visitors to Knole were being charged two shillings each to be shown round, adding a useful £3,000 a year to the estate income.

Borrowings taken out at times when income looked secure and far-off repayments could virtually be guaranteed landed heavily on the shoulders of later generations who faced unpalatable choices. 'Some little time ago a shrewd young peer,' writes Nevill in the 1920s, 'after succeeding to the family estates, at once proceeded to sell everything he could, including the portraits of his ancestors, amongst them that of his grandfather, which drew forth remonstrances from some of his friends. "I have good reasons to sell the old gentleman," said he, "for like other people he must pay his debts. When he was in control of the property he mortgaged it to the extent of no less than a good many thousands, which I find myself obliged to pay off.

It is only natural, therefore, that he should be made to do what he can to make amends for his reckless extravagance and help me to find the money. Even now the old man still owes me a good bit, for unfortunately his portrait fetched only two hundred pounds."'

This is just one example of a pattern of retrenchment and rethinking repeated in historic houses everywhere – one that called for fresh ideas and new horizons – but it was by no means a cry of universal despair. As long ago as 1903, the then Countess of Warwick published a history of Warwick Castle and its Earls and concluded by looking back down the centuries from what today seems like the enchanted Edwardian era, in which she lived.

'We have tried – both Lord Warwick and myself – to adapt the ancient Castle to the needs of the present day, to blend the old and the new, and, while continuing its historic traditions, to make the Castle the centre of many movements for the benefit of others – not only those among whom our immediate lot is cast, but the nation at large. For Warwick Castle is a national glory as well as a personal possession, and we, who hold it now, strive to fulfil, imperfectly it may be, the duties of

Warwick Castle in its Edwardian heyday.

our stewardship and the privileges of our heritage. To chronicle all the gatherings which have taken place at Warwick Castle since 1893 would be to weary and not to edify. But as a proof that our idea of hospitality has not been a narrow one, I may mention various assemblies there of interesting groups of men and women, such as trades-unionists, co-operators, educationists, women agriculturists, cab-drivers, pen-workers, yeomanry, Colonial Premiers, Colonial cricketers, and Colonial troops. We have more than once had the honour of entertaining his present Majesty King Edward VII, at the time when he was Prince of Wales, and other members of the Royal Family. I may also record that Lord Warwick has been on several occasions Mayor of the Borough of Warwick, and that our son, Lord Brooke, has served his country during the South African War. All this will go to prove that at Warwick Castle the old has touched hands with the new.

'For times have greatly changed since the days of the most interesting events related in my history. We are a long way from the old conception of an Earl as a man who, in time of peace, should gather in the third pennies of the counties, and in time of war should marshal his tenants in battle-array, now to fight the King's enemies, and now to determine his own private quarrels …

'On the other hand, the altered circumstances have brought new duties, new responsibilities, new opportunities, to the owners of Warwick Castle, as to all the world. One is in touch with life at more points; there is an opening for the exercise of broader sympathies; one can do good by organising as well as by almsgiving. Moreover, the modern conditions are such that women are no longer debarred from bearing their share in the work that waits to be done for the amelioration of the world. A woman's life may nowadays reasonably be fuller, more interesting, and more useful than in the past.'

If Lady Warwick was laying down a marker to future generations of historic house owners, it was one that that many would recognise and act upon.

Major James More-Molyneux was one of many young men returning to civilian life at end of the

Second World War who found themselves exchanging one struggle for survival for another. Now it was the ravages of time, not tyranny, that had to be faced up to if the houses and estates that their parents had managed to keep going through wartime shortages and rationing were not going to be lost in the years of austerity that soon extinguished the glow which peace had brought in 1945.

For Major More-Molyneux, the challenge he faced lay in Loseley Park, near Guildford in Surrey; the home where his family has lived since the reign of Queen Elizabeth I. 'Each generation of the family is called upon to serve Loseley in its own particular way,' he writes in his book *The Loseley Challenge*. 'One builds, another pulls down; some make money, others spend. My parents' role during those very difficult and uncomfortable war years was probably the hardest. Electricity had not yet been laid on, there was no heating, as the boilers were out of commission, so there was no piped hot water; if you wanted a bath you put the kettle

Early nineteenth-century Loseley Park when the lawn was still mown by a gardener wielding a scythe.

23

on the kitchen stove and carried it up to the bathroom.

'The house was always extremely cold in winter, with vast areas of windows, the wind whistling through the leaded diamond panes. I remember particularly the scullery: washing up in there in the bitter cold was a nightmare …

'I cannot emphasise sufficiently the debt that I owe, and that Loseley owes, to my parents for staying in the House during that desperately uncomfortable period of the war and, despite their need of money, refusing to sell any land or contents of the House. That supreme unselfishness strengthened my resolve to ensure that Loseley should survive and be worthy of them.'

After demobilsation in April 1946, he set to, aided from October 1948 by his wife Sue and a small team of dedicated workers. From his childhood James More-Molyneux had always wanted to run his own business; now he had the chance and he seized the opportunity. 'After demob I soon began to get a grip of things as evinced by my notebook dated July 1946, headed "Planning". Details include

"building and contracting, conversion of own timber, lathe turning, canning tomato ketchup etc, lavender growing and processing, horse chestnut meal processing. *Marketing* – advertising. Retail own milk. Shop and milk bar. Canning, drying apples. Potatoes – get contract and dig earlies early. *Forestry* – planting programme, trainees, portable saw for logs, charcoal, saw benches re-bedded, steam engine for rack bench. *Estate* – list of all properties showing repairs, building programme. *Farm* – removal of dead trees, bushes, brambles, drainage plan for fields (scheme completed with grant aid 1947). Gates and posts, paint all buildings and machinery. Eradicate weeds. Roadways." There were several detailed improvements for the cows [Loseley has long been famous for its herd of Jerseys] including "more food – how? more fields? grazing corn in spring, rye grass as catch crop. *Office* – calving chart, cropping programme, field manuring and cropping sheet, costings, timesheets, milk graph, cow feeding charts, bull progeny list".'

Sixty years on, the day-to-day running of Loseley has passed to Major More-Molyneux's son, Michael and his wife Sarah, though Major More-Molyneux still takes an active interest in everything going on. Asked to describe his father's attributes, Michael replies, 'I would say he is an entrepreneur – always into new ideas. He just has a feel for what's right, what's wrong, what's going to make a go and what isn't … He's very switched on, Dad – thirty years ahead of his time.'

It didn't take Michael's father long to realise that growing a little wheat and barley wouldn't provide the level of income needed to undertake the huge restoration programme that Loseley required. Clearly an inspired entrepreneur, Major

More-Molyneux hit on the idea of supplying flagpoles for the Coronation in 1953, making use of timber on the estate. From this he moved into the construction business, producing concrete blocks and pre-fabricated houses.

Michael More-Molyneux's grandfather had founded the famous Loseley Jersey Herd in 1916 and drove the milk round himself delivering to customers. Michael's father built up this estate-based business, forming Loseley Dairy Products in 1968. 'We commenced with the production of cheese, followed by yoghourt and the ice cream,' his son explains. 'At peak we were supplying some

1,500 customers in London and the Home Counties, exporting to the Far East, Middle East and also Italy, and our customers included Harrods, Fortnum & Mason's, British Airways and the Royal Opera House to name but a few.'

In 1985 overseas competition and the lack of land on which to expand led the family to sell the Dairy Products business. The former yoghourt and ice cream production buildings are now rented to a variety of businesses. 'An architect has got an office here,' Michael says. 'We've got a sale room, a landscape gardener's headquarters. The children's charity CHASE are next door to us. A Thai restaurant has got two warehouses here. We've found that in this area there are a lot of people who want in the region of 1,000 square feet of office space … They don't have to be in a high street.' With no parking problems and rents lower than those charged in nearby Guildford, the redundant commercial buildings at Loseley are ideal for start-up businesses. And there can be few more agreeable places to work than on a 400-year-old estate, surrounded by pastures, cornfields and stands of mature trees.

This pattern of enterprise, of building on the strengths of an historic estate, of utilising redundant buildings and facilities to grow new businesses, can be seen everywhere. Self-evidently, the most visible assets of any such estate are its house and the gardens and parkland in which it sits. Here is Michael More-Molyneux again, describing the breadth of tourism and hospitality-based business that has been developed at Loseley, which will be familiar to historic houses and their owners up and down the country. 'We welcome some 130,000 visitors to Loseley a year, who will either come to visit the House and Gardens or to attend one of our major events. Weddings are becoming increasingly popular and we expect to cater for eighty wedding receptions and thirty-five civil ceremonies a year, as well as hosting numerous corporate activities, family celebrations, and the odd film! Our larger events include a gardening show, craft fair, dog show, open air concert and ploughing match/country fair.'

As President of the Historic Houses Association, James Hervey-Bathurst has a good overview of

the variety of initiatives undertaken by the association's 350 or so member properties that are regularly open to the public on a commercial basis. Employing upwards of 10,000 people and contributing an estimated £1.6–£2 billion to the economy, these properties collectively represent a very significant element of the present-day rural economy.

James Hervey-Bathurst's own family home, Eastnor Castle in Herefordshire, illustrates the turnaround that many estates have experienced in the course of three generations. He explains that a lot of land

was sold by his family between 1883 and 1920, reducing the size of the Eastnor estate from 13,000 acres to a third of its former size. 'The estate has always been underfunded, in terms of the buildings it has to repair and the income it has to repair them,' he points out. Though he adds that higher levels of rental income today mean that it is now feasible to invest, say, £50,000 in refurbishing an estate cottage and recoup that outlay in ten to fifteen years.

'That is a big change in my life time,' James continues. 'Before you couldn't do it. My parents

therefore had to sell off cottages. They were not economically viable.'

Another very significant change that has taken place has been the growth of leisure activities over the last decades. The Eastnor accounts show that income from leisure activities (excluding shooting) has risen to fifteen times its former level. 'Rents have gone up five times,' James continues, 'woodlands have declined, farming has gone up by a third only. Repairs and maintenance expenditure has gone up from less than £60,000 to over £400,000. Office expenses and employment expenses have gone up from £20,000 to £300,000. Turnover has gone up six times since 1986.'

To emphasise the shift away from traditional forms of estate income to new ones, he quotes the employment statistics, 'Where we used to employ ten people on the farm, we now employ one and use part-timers when we need them. Where we employed three people in the house, we now employ eight.'

Other employment opportunities, not directly connected to the estate, but locally based, have

also come about as a result of well-targeted investment. 'The Castle hasn't had all the investment in the last few years,' James says. 'It has had a lot of it, but the rest has gone into other properties. For example, we had no commercial rents twenty years ago and now twenty per cent of our rental income is

Major roof repairs at Eastnor Castle illustrating the daunting scale of conservation and maintenance work that owners of historic houses constantly face.

commercial. We've grown that through investment and the help of grants. DEFRA and the Regional Development Agency and its predecessor have been prepared to put money into converting buildings where new jobs will be created in the countryside. So we often have a virtuous situation where we get a grant, we have retained our low-cost housing so that people who want to work here are occasionally able to rent a cottage to walk or bicycle to work, because they're employed where they live.'

While weddings and corporate hospitality represent a significant portfolio of new business enterprises for a great many historic houses, most have some special feature, or features (unique selling points in marketing terms), that they have been able to develop – and in some cases these reflect personal interests of owners past and present.

James Hervey-Bathurst's father had a keen interest in agricultural engineering, from which he became particularly interested in Land-Rovers. As a consequence, Land-Rover engineers received a warm and enthusiastic reception thirty years ago, when they were offered the chance to test drive their vehicles on the Eastnor estate, where muddy woodland tracks and very steep hills on the flanks

of the Malverns provide an ideal range of challenging terrain for both vehicles and drivers. The construction of the first stretch of the M42 some years later created a direct motorway link between the Land-Rover factory in Solihull and Eastnor, which made the test facilities there even more attractive. These were enhanced by the proximity of the Castle, which provided a perfect venue for entertaining major Land-Rover clients in the home and export markets. In 1987 a formalised contract was drawn up and today the company has a permanent office on the estate that looks after vehicle testing and off-road driving tuition.

What began as a personal interest a generation ago has grown into what James Hervey-Bathurst describes as a 'very happy arrangement', from which the estate not only derives an annual income but also an additional facility to offer to corporate clients, who are increasingly seeing Eastnor as a major team-building venue.

Like many historic houses, Eastnor Castle has a deer park and this too has proved to be an important venue, for a three-day pop festival, The Big Chill, that is staged every August. Once again, good road connections and a willingness on the part of the owner and his team to work with the promoter to provide the right facilities has resulted in an annual event that makes a useful contribution to estate income.

James Hervey-Bathurst is not alone in developing the commercial potential of his family home on what he describes as a 'suck it and see basis'. 'My parents had set it up well with Land-Rover and we worked in stages from that. If we'd put a business plan together, it wouldn't have stacked up. It's a danger. If you look at a house like this and say it needs a new central heating system, electricity, plumbing, fire prevention, roof insulation, etc., etc. – you come up with such a huge sum of money that you end up having to have a sale to pay for it. What prompted it here, was that the top of the house – the keep – was beginning to fall down. Water was getting in and it was bulging out. So English Heritage offered us a grant and we had to match fund it by fifty per cent. That prompted us to get going. The grants saved us from selling contents, and it helped that I was employed off the estate at that time. As grants are now much reduced, it will be harder for owners in the future to do their major repairs.'

His account could be repeated in any number of estate offices and elegant drawing-rooms of historic houses; the individual circumstances may be different, but the fundamental challenges that faced the two post-war generations of owning families are broadly the same across a broad swathe of stately homes.

Many present-day owners, who saw the inspiring renovation work undertaken by their parents, have carried this forward, at the same time establishing a level of sustainable business

ventures that are giving their estates a degree of financial stability their parents could only wish for. Mrs Clare Macpherson-Grant Russell is the twenty-second generation of her family (and the first 'Lady Laird') to live at their beautiful home, Ballindalloch Castle in Banffshire, set in the magnificent surroundings of the Spey valley in the Highlands of Scotland. For her, Ballindalloch has been a much-cherished family home since she was five years old, even though life in her early days there was far from the comfort enjoyed by her family and guests today.

'It was a complete and utter nightmare,' she recalls. 'There was no proper central heating, there was no proper electricity; the lights fizzed every time you put them on. And there was one bathroom in the whole place, with half a bath full of water, which you shared with about five other people. Also, when it rained, you had to have buckets everywhere.'

She goes on to say, however, 'Fortunately my parents had the foresight in about 1965 to redo the castle from top to toe. We were out of it for three solid years and we probably had about ten tradesmen working every day. They redid the entire house and put in ten bathrooms. They re-roofed. They put in central heating. They had to take down twelve rooms and build the gable up again. And it all came to just under £20,000! We found the accounts quite recently.

'Now we are doing one side of the house: chimneys, dormer windows, taking down stone ornaments and renovating them – and I think two dormer windows is about the same cost as the entire castle between 1965 and 1968.'

In the corridor leading to the nursery at Ballindalloch are pictures of the Castle painted by the Laird when she was a child. The nursery itself represents a history of 'young lairds and lasses from the late eighteenth century'.

It isn't only this disparity in costs that contrasts the running and maintenance of Ballindalloch today with a generation ago. When Mrs Macpherson-Grant Russell's parents needed to pay for work on the castle, they sold land on the margins of the estate to cover it. Today, thanks in large measure to the financial expertise of her banker husband, Oliver, current expenditure is covered by the profits generated by a variety of successful hospitality enterprises.

'When we arrived here [in 1978],' his wife will tell you, 'we could afford to pay one person. We had £20,000 coming in.'

Since then they have built up a lucrative business entertaining house parties in the Castle itself and offering fully-staffed accommodation in a number of estate properties. In addition to the lure of staying in one of the most beautiful and romantic castles in Scotland, guests can enjoy the traditional activities of a Highland sporting estate: fishing, shooting and stalking, with the bonus of playing golf on Ballindalloch's own course on the banks of the River Avon.

Add to these income from a windfarm, which in her husband's words 'gives us a known position, index-linked for twenty-five years', and it has been possible to put in place a maintenance fund to take forward the programme of work that an estate of this size calls for. 'There is absolutely no problem with Highland estates,' Oliver Russell maintains, 'as long as you have money coming in and spend that. But there is no way that you can gear up as you would on other property projects in other parts of the world and be happy that you can be in a safe position.'

Being in a safe position is not something that Sir Thomas Ingilby would have laid claim to when he inherited Ripley Castle, his family's ancestral home in North Yorkshire, where the Ingilbys have lived since the early fourteenth century. Barely six weeks into his army career, his father died wholly unexpectedly at the age of just sixty-seven. Sir Thomas's father had effectively been given Ripley Castle and its estate on his wedding day and thereafter employed an agent to manage it for him. He and Sir Thomas's mother lived on the first floor of the Castle, while his

Fishing today on the Ballindalloch beats can be as rewarding as it was for previous generations of house guests.

parents occupied the ground floor. At that time the Castle was open to visitors one day a week, on Sunday afternoons – though as Sir Thomas mentions, 'If friends came round to tea, the Castle was unceremoniously closed.'

When Sir Thomas found himself holding the reins in 1974, the estate amounted to around 3,500 acres, divided into fifteen farms, all of them on fixed rents. However, Sir Thomas's responsibilities were not restricted to a sizeable Castle that dated back to the Middle Ages and fifteen farmsteads all in need of urgent repair: he also had the village of Ripley, which nestles around the Castle, to take care of – and among the properties here were four houses on annual rents of less than fifty pounds a year.

'The rents were fixed,' Sir Thomas explains. 'We couldn't increase them even if we had wanted to because they were effectively blocked. The houses were run down, so the rent was low. But as we couldn't increase the rent we couldn't afford to spend any money on the properties. So it really was a vicious circle.'

Sir Thomas had always known that the responsibility of taking care of Ripley would one day be his, but he hadn't expected to be facing the challenge fresh out of school. With his military career summarily curtailed, he changed tacks totally and studied land management at agricultural college, alongside gaining practical experience, working first on a local farm and later with two firms of land agents.

'The trouble was he [Sir Thomas's father] hadn't survived the seven-year period that he needed to live for the settlement to become tax efficient, so we got caught right the way down the line. Within a few months of his dying, Estate Duty gave way to Capital Transfer Tax and Capital Gains Tax. So we got caught by all three regimes, and eventually had to pay Capital Gains Tax on the land we sold to pay the Estate Duty and Capital Transfer Tax.'

Guided by their very helpful family solicitor and a land agent, for whom he later went to work, Sir Thomas felt far from overawed by the responsibilities facing him. 'At the age of eighteen you think you can do anything,' he cheerfully says.

'The world is your oyster and you don't appreciate the risks involved at that stage.'

These were not inconsiderable. For the next seven years the estate paid everything it earned to the exchequer. 'We were aware of all these properties that needed renovating. We were aware of the scope that we had here, but we couldn't afford to invest in the properties, to do the upgrading that they needed.' In addition land and properties on the periphery of the estate had to be sold off to help meet the tax bill.

Sir Thomas's mother remained living in the Castle and having been one of her son's trustees she was closely involved in the running of the estate in his early years. Even so, Sir Thomas acknowledges 'it

Picturesque as it always has been, Ripley village has been an added burden of responsibility for owners of the Castle since its remodelling in the first half of the nineteenth century.

was very difficult for anyone of her generation to really appreciate how the world was changing and how we needed to evolve, to change with it.'

Difficult it may have been, but Lady Diana Ingilby threw her weight behind the changes that would transform Ripley's fortunes over the next thirty years. Small groups of visiting Americans, paying fourteen pounds for a light lunch and twenty-two pounds for a full dinner, began to call at Ripley Castle from the mid-1970s. A newspaper article in the early 1980s noted, 'Lady Diana Ingilby presides over the American receptions, and helps to cook

the food . . . a job she confesses is "always quite nerve-racking".'

Sir Thomas, aged twenty-five at the time the article was written, was full of ideas and optimism: 'I feel that stately homes have enormous potential and it's really a question of finding enterprises that fit in well.'

Among the enterprises he had in mind a quarter of a century ago were 'converting the decrepit

Throwing open the doors makes headline news.

game larders into self-catering units, building shops in the stables, and opening a banqueting room for conferences and weddings.' Given a few small adjustments, this is almost exactly what he and his wife, Lady Emma have achieved.

In some respects necessity made Ripley Castle one of the pioneers in offering paid hospitality to visitors and external clients. After the engagement was announced between the Prince of Wales and Lady Diana Spencer in February 1981, the same press article that featured Sir Thomas and Ripley's own Lady Diana, gleefully reported, 'A right royal rumpus blew up this week over reports that the Earl and Countess of Spencer – parents of Prince Charles's bride-to-be – were inviting American tourists to lunch to cover the costs of their Northamptonshire home [Althorp].'

Sir Thomas is honest enough to admit that thirty years ago the idea was totally alien, even to him. 'I remember going to an Historic Houses

41

Association meeting in London shortly after I had inherited and hearing about a house in Kent that took companies into their drawing room for conferences. I thought they were completely and utterly mad: both the house owners and the companies. I couldn't imagine why a company wanted to use a stately home and why the stately home owners would want the companies and how they would cater for them. I remember thinking that could never happen at Ripley, we simply didn't have the facilities to do that. It was just a dream – totally beyond us.'

Three decades, a lot of nail biting, years of hard work and well over £3,500,000 later that dream is now a thriving, prosperous reality. As Sir Thomas modestly puts it, a change in tax legislation that allowed companies to offset corporate hospitality against Corporation Tax suddenly created a new market that simply hadn't existed before. Taxation had forced many owners of historic houses to search for new sources of sustainable income and here was taxation creating what amounted to a completely untapped business opportunity. Ripley Castle was one of many moving quickly into the burgeoning corporate hospitality market, where they have established themselves as key venues and, in the process, introduced a new income stream to the balance sheets of their estates.

Another piece of legislation that has had a far-reaching effect in improving the income of many historic houses was the Marriage Act 1995, which permitted couples to be married in a civil ceremony at licensed venues, rather than at register offices. This allowed stately homes to obtain a licence and enter the lucrative wedding market, offering a matchless venue for a wedding reception and now an equally memorable location for the civil wedding itself. In the decade that has passed since the act came into being, weddings have made a significant contribution to the annual income of hundreds of historic houses – and from this has stemmed business and job opportunities in the wider rural economy for all manner of wedding 'providers': from caterers and car hire firms to printers and photographers.

Sir Brooke Boothby is another of the current generation of historic house owners who have

Fonmon Castle in
South Wales.

built successful hospitality businesses in their ancestral homes. He is also one who had to cope with the very heavy burden of taxation, which in his case was brought about by the untimely death of not one, but both of his parents.

Added to these difficulties that faced Fonmon Castle, the Boothby family home in the Vale of Glamorgan in South Wales, in the early 1990s, was a legacy of financial difficulties that had seen the estate eroded by previous, profligate generations. Two centuries earlier a predecessor had gambled away Barry Island, losing that portion of the Fonmon estate in one night racing snails!

Move forward to the twentieth century and Sir Brooke's grandfather had to deal with a major family row over who should inherit Fonmon and other family assets. This resulted in the need to buy back parts of the estate. So when Sir Brooke's father inherited in 1951 he discovered, in his son's words 'that the place is mortgaged to the hilt. He actually had to sell a silver teapot to survive the first three months paying the estate staff ... They struggled. But he was a banker and a successful man, and as a result he did a fantastic amount

here. He got the whole place rewired. He put central heating in.'

Each of the last three owners of Fonmon has made a significant contribution to securing its financial well-being. Sir Brooke's grandfather started a quarrying business. Sir Brooke's father created the large caravan park. And now Sir Brooke has masterminded the opening of the Castle for weddings, private functions and a range of corporate events.

Although most historic house owners are wary of long-term, itemised development and maintenance schemes, Sir Brooke has a very definite plan of action. 'My target is that the major rococo changes here were finished in 1762 and I would like by 2012 to have it back to where it was when they'd finished those changes.' Indeed, he is a strong advocate of forward planning, based in part on the experience of his own inheritance.

'The worst part at a macro level was definitely my mother contracting leukaemia,' he says. 'She was ten years young than my father. So we thought we could hand it to her, there'd be time for her to hand it to me, live seven years and we'd get away.

It failed. Having had a substantive six-figure cash sum to find after my father's death, we then had to find an equal and slightly higher one for my mother's death. That wiped out every single piece of family investment. But we held on to the land and the contents.' And they provided the foundation for the turnaround in Fonmon's fortunes that Sir Brooke has overseen.

He had the opportunity to study the critical importance of looking ahead and making proper provision for the handover of a historic house and estate during his time as chairman of the succession committee of the Historic Houses Association. 'It was an interesting exercise,' he recalls. 'We watched some spectacular disagreements between fathers and sons. We also ran a computer exercise for a family with a middle-sized country house (about forty or fifty rooms). We gave them about 3,000 acres, a family company with good solid turnover, no divorce, no sudden two-generation deaths in five years. But, we gave them the one major handicap: they had made no provision for succession at all. They just let things roll on and then the death duties came.'

The result of this exercise?

'The whole lot wiped out in four generations. Gone in eighty years, under the tax laws as they were thirty years ago.'

'I think it would still hold true today,' he maintains. 'If you do nothing, the tax bills will defeat the earning ability.'

In layman's terms, the owner of a historic house needs to hand over to the next generation early enough and then live seven years. It's not dissimilar to the advice financial advisors give to all their clients – to make a will. Without forward-thinking provision, the delicate financial balance – even of properties with well-run, productive businesses – would be unable to sustain the seismic impact of tax payments.

Over the last hundred years much may have changed in the way that historic houses sustain themselves financially, but the importance of foresight and judicious planning are as essential today as they were when the founders of these great houses and estates set down their dynastic roots centuries ago.

45

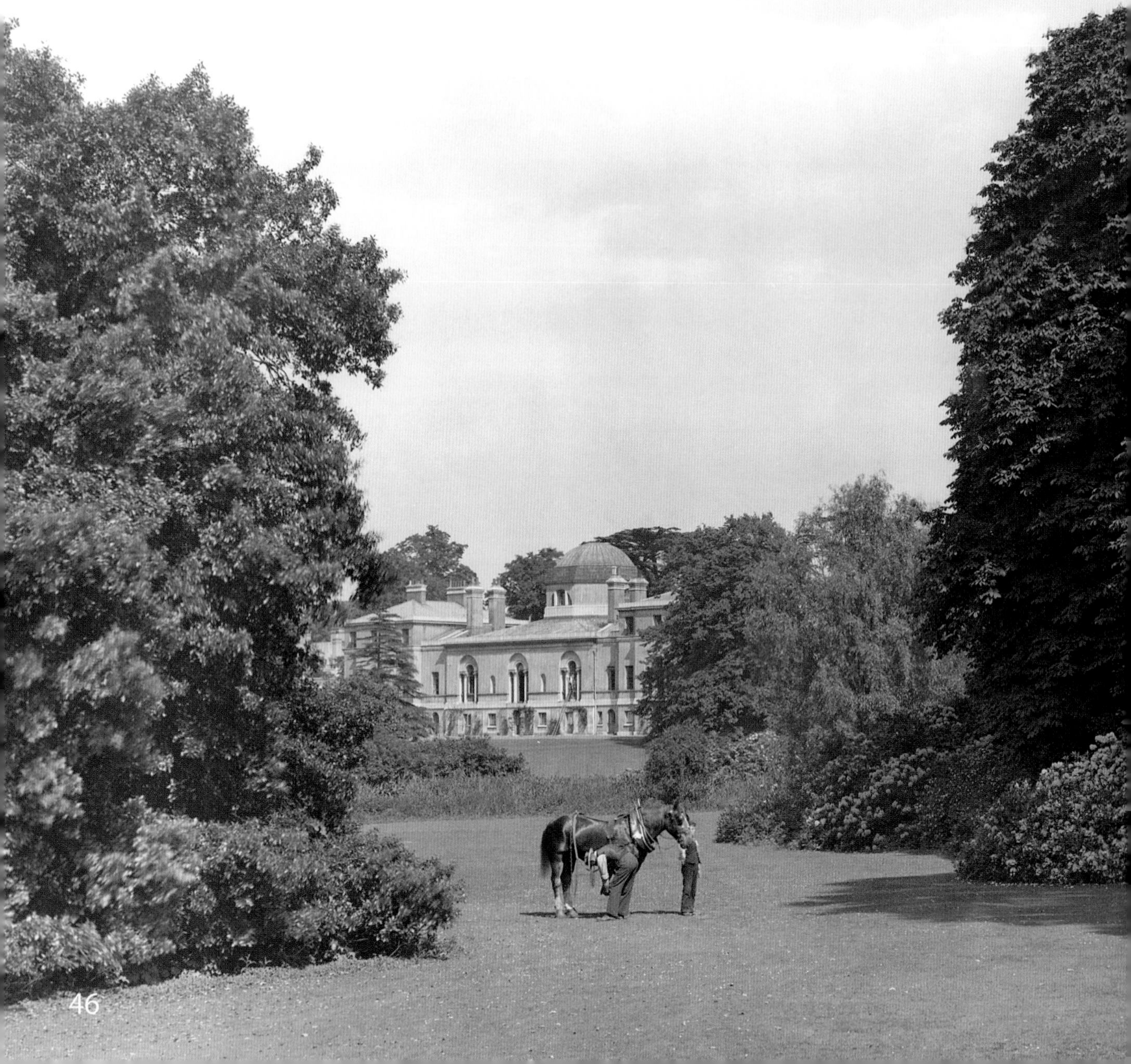

Living over the Shop

For the most part historic houses were originally constructed to provide places where their owners, their families and those they invited to join them, could spend their days in tranquil isolation. Surrounded and buttressed by their large estates, they were largely free to do as they pleased, and for several generations it was not uncommon for little attention to be given to the income needed to support their way of life. Occasionally horrendous debts (often resulting from reckless gambling) might necessitate the sale of substantial holdings of land, if not an entire estate, but for much of the eighteenth and early nineteenth centuries the landed gentry were able to enjoy the privacy and privilege their station in life afforded them, free from the concerns of the wider world, free too from the sizeable tax burdens that would fall on their descendants.

Life in the eighteenth century
at Badminton House.

An account of life in the household of the Duke of Beaufort at Badminton, at the end of the seventeenth century, gives a vivid example of stately living in past centuries. The occasion described was a week-long visit made by Lord Guildford, who was a distant relative of the Duke's, and it was recorded by the Hon Roger North, who was also a member of the family.

'I mention this entertainment,' his account of the visit begins, 'as a handle of showing a princely way of living, which that noble duke used, above any other except crowned heads, that I have had notice of in Europe; and, in some respects, greater than most of them, to whom he might have made an example. He had above £2000 per annum in his hands, which he managed by stewards, bailiffs, and servants; and, of that, a great part of the country, which was his own lying round about him, was part, and the husbandmen, etc., were of his family [i.e. household], and provided for in his large expanded house. He bred all his horses, which came to the husbandry first colts, and from thence, as they were fit, were taken into his equipage; and, as by age or accident they grew unfit for that

service, they were returned to the place from whence they came and there expired; except what, for plenty or unfitness, were sold or disposed of. He had about two hundred persons in his family, all provided for; and in his capital house, nine original tables covered every day: and, for the accommodation of so many, a large hall was built, with a sort of alcove at one end, for distinction; but yet the whole lay in the view of him that was chief, who had the power to do what was proper for keeping order amongst them; and it was his charge to see it done. The tables were properly assigned; as, for example, the chief steward with the gentlemen and pages; the master of the horse with the coachmen and liveries; an under steward with the bailiffs and some husbandmen; the clerk of the kitchen with the bakers, brewers, etc. all together; and other more inferior people, under these, in places apart. The women had their dining-room also, and were distributed in like manner. My lady's chief woman with the gentlewomen; the housekeeper with the maids and some others. The method of governing this great family was admirable and easy, and such as might have been a pattern for any management whatever. For if the duke or duchess (who concerned herself much more than he did; for every day of her life in the morning she took her tour and visited every office about the house, and was her own superintendent) observed anything amiss or suspicious, as a servant riding out or the like, nothing was said to that servant; but his immediate superior, or one of a higher order, was sent for who was to inquire and answer if leave had been given or not; if not, such servant was straight turned away. No fault of order was passed by; for it may be concluded there are enough of them that pass undiscovered. All the provisions of the family came from foreign parts as merchandise. Soap and candle were made in the house; so likewise the malt was ground there; and all the drink that came to the duke's table, was of malt sun-dried upon the leads of his house …

'As for the duke and duchess, and their friends, there was no time of the day without diversion. Breakfast in her gallery that opened into the gardens; then, perhaps, a deer was to be killed, or the gardens, and parks with the several sorts of deer, to be visited; and if it required mounting, horses of the duke's were brought for all the company. And so, in the afternoon, when the ladies were disposed to air, and the gentlemen with them, coaches and six came to hold them all. At half an hour after eleven the bell rang to prayers, so at six in the evening; and, through a gallery, the best company went into an aisle in the church (so near it was), and the duke and duchess could see if all the family were there. The ordinary pastime of the ladies was in a gallery on the other side, where she had divers gentlewomen commonly at work upon embroidery and fringe-making; for all the beds of state were made and finished in the house. The meats were very neat, and not gross; no servants in livery attended, but those called gentlemen only; and in several kinds, even down to the small beer, nothing could be more choice than the table was. It was an oblong, and not an oval; and the duchess, with two daughters only, sat at the upper end. If the gentleman chose a glass of wine, the civil offers were made either to go down to the vaults, which were very large and sumptuous, or servants at a sign given, attended with salvers, etc., and many a brisk round went about; but no sitting at a table with tobacco and healths, as the too common use is. And this way of entertaining continues a week, while we were there, with incomparable variety; for the duke had always some new project of building, walling, or planting, which he would show, and ask his friends their advice about; and nothing was forced, or strained, but easy and familiar, as if it was, and really so I thought it to be, the common course and way of living of that family …'

Eighteenth-century guests of Lord Egremont at Petworth in Sussex enjoyed a pleasantly chaotic existence in which they were able to do pretty much as they pleased. The Georgian diarist Thomas Creevey went to Petworth and recorded, 'How we got into the house, I don't quite recollect, for I think there was no bell, but I know we were some time at the door and when we were let in by a little footman he disappeared *de suite* and it was some time before we saw anybody else …

'Lord Egremont received his guests with the utmost urbanity and courtesy, did the honours of his table and in every other respect left them free to abide as long as they pleased. Petworth was consequently like a great inn. Everybody came when they thought fit and departed without notice of leaving. He liked to have people there who he was certain would not put him out of his way, especially those who, entering into his eccentricities, were ready for snatches of talk which his perpetual locomotion alone permitted of and from who he could gather information about passing events; but it was necessary to conform to his peculiarities and these were utterly incompatible with conversation or any prolonged discussion. He never remained for five minutes in the same place and was continually oscillating between the library and his bedroom, or wandering about the enormous house in all directions.'

Until his death in 1827 the Duke of York 'dispensed much lavish hospitality to the fashionable world', according to a social commentator a century later. 'The Oatlands Park "week-ends" brought together … every one who was anybody, and shortly before five o'clock p.m.

there started from White's Club, in St James's, a string of chaises so long as to monopolize much of that fashionable thoroughfare – the arrival of the procession at Oatlands must have been a picturesque as well as an amusing sight.'

After-dinner entertainment for Regency guests at some stately homes took on a more boisterous air than the image created by Jane Austen's writings might suggest. An example of what could occur was given in 1812 by Lady Frances Shelley, who was staying at Woburn Abbey where, 'a formal reception prepared the way for a silent dinner of twenty people … During dinner everyone whispered to his next neighbour, and I was obliged to do the same, from the dread of hearing my own voice. But when evening came, God knows, I had no longer the same fear, for a scene of such vulgar noise and riot I never beheld.

'As soon as we left the dining room, the Duchess [of Bedford] went to her nursing employment (after a little edifying conversation of the subject) and we dispersed into different parties, through an *enfilade* of six rooms. The gentlemen soon joined us, and in the first Shelley got a companion at billiards. In the next Lady Asgill established herself in an attitude, lying on a sofa with Sir Thomas Graham at her feet. In the next, a sober rubber at whist. In the next, Lady Jane and Miss Russell at a harp, and in the long gallery a few pairs were dispersed on the sofas; others sauntered from room to room. I joined the latter and talked of furniture, china and ormolu till the subject was exhausted … at last, I established myself at a writing table in the card-room. Scarcely was I seated, when the Duchess entered; and collecting her romping force of girls and young men they all seized cushions and began pelting the whist players. They defended themselves by throwing the cards and candles at her head; but the Duchess succeeded in over throwing the table and a regular battle ensued with cushions, oranges and apples. The romp was at last ended by Lady Jane being nearly blinded by an apple that hit her in the eye. Shelly, before

that, had been nearly smothered by the female romps getting him to the ground and pummelling him with cushions. To this succeeded Blind Man's Buff. I stole off to bed.'

As a child the future Queen Victoria made regular visits to country houses with her mother the Duchess of Kent. One of her visits was to the Old Palace Mayfield, and the preparations it occasioned

Queen Victoria pictured in 1823 when she was four years old.

were recorded by a fellow guest, Mrs Day, who lived in nearby Hadlow. Writing to her son, she explained how the invitation amounted to something of a royal command: 'Your Father had a note from Lord Delawarr,' began her letter, 'who had previously promised to bring Lady Delawarr with him to the ruins, where we were to have a luncheon prepared. The Duchess of Kent was staying at Tunbridge Wells, and this note stated that the plan was changed, that the subject had been mentioned at the Duchess' table, and that he had been desired to give the Duchess' commands to your Father to attend her there on the following day, and that it would be proper (though not imperative) that I should accompany him.

'At the hour fixed, or rather about half an hour earlier, we were on the spot. Instead of its usual quiet, it was filled with servants bringing in everything necessary for the collation, or as Mrs Homewood (the farmer's wife, who had charge of the place) said, "There were nasty furriners jabbering everywhere." Soon Lord and Lady Delawarr arrived to do the honours. Just then arrived the Duchess, the Princess, and their suite.

Lord Delawarr and his family being a quarter of an hour after time, it was very awkward, as we did not know one person. The appearance of the whole "cortège" was not imposing; such a dusty party I think I have never seen ... A call for a clothes' brush followed, and after considerable delay it was procured, and the young ladies set to work to brush each other's habits at the door of the sitting room. This did away with a good deal of the ceremony, and occasioned much fun. The Princess Victoria was then about fourteen or fifteen years of age, and I heard her say that it was not the first time that she had visited Mayfield; that on the previous occasion she was quite a little child; that she had fallen asleep in the carriage, and awoke very hungry, adding, "I never was so angry in my life; there was nothing to be had that I could eat." You will, perhaps, like to know the names of those who were there. I remember the Baroness Leitzen (I am not sure that the name is exactly correct); the Princess' governess Dr Davies, then her tutor; Miss Davies; Sir John and Lady Conroy, and two daughters; Lady Flora Hastings (for whose very kind attention I had much reason to be obliged, for your father was called upon to act as cicerone, and when luncheon had been discussed, I was the only person not known to all, and should have been uncomfortable, had she not joined me). There were some others in the Duchess' suite, but I have forgotten their names. Lord and Lady Delawarr were also there with their eldest daughter and the youngest, the Present Marchioness of Salisbury. She was a little girl then, and the princess delighted her by presenting her with a silver-mounted riding whip.'

Crowned and married, her royal visits took on a more formal atmosphere, as the *Warwickshire Advertiser* duly recorded when Queen Victoria and Prince Albert paid a visit to Warwick Castle in June 1858: 'Her Majesty was received by the Earl and Countess of Warwick, accompanied by Lord Brooke (who presented the Queen with a beautiful bouquet) and the masters Greville. These juvenile members of Lord Warwick's family were each saluted by Her Majesty, as well as by most of the distinguished visitors, and their pleasing appearance attracted the notice of every one present. The Royal party immediately went to the State rooms, after inspecting which they partook of luncheon in the Banqueting-room. The table was loaded with profuse rarities, and the most costly and elegant gold service. There were twenty-eight chairs of antique pattern, trimmed with fine old brocade. Upon two magnificent sideboards were ranged a superb display of the pieces of plate won by his lordship's horses. One of these, a beautiful salver, was run for at Liverpool in 1845, and was given for turf competition to commemorate the zeal displayed by the Lord George Bentinck in suppressing malpractices on the turf. The State chair was a richly gilded frame, cushioned and backed with crimson silk velvet.

'Whilst the Royal and illustrious guests were partaking of Earl Warwick's hospitality in the Grand Saloon, the humbler people in the Castle were not neglected. The cellars were open for the servants and *attachés* of all the visitors, and the most considerate and unbounded entertainment was afforded to those who needed it.

'Subsequently the Royal party went over the Castle grounds, and Her Majesty graciously visited the recently erected additions to the Castle, and made various enquiries as to the use of the several new parts. Prince Albert, who was dressed and looked like a good English gentleman, quietly observed the many valuable armorial relics and paid great attention to many of the artistic treasures with which the rooms abound. Back again to the courtyard, the Queen again took the Earl of Warwick's arm and slowly walked across the fine lawn, upon which the Yeomanry band was stationed. As the Queen and the Earl passed down the lawn, Her Majesty enquired for the Prince Consort, and was informed that his Royal Highness was climbing the famous Guy Tower. The Queen then passed on under the beautiful cedars, elms, yews, and other trees, until her arrival at the Greenhouse, in which is the celebrated 'Warwick Vase'. Here were two reporters from illustrated London papers and our own representative, whose presence was graciously permitted by Her Majesty. Prince Albert having descended from the Tower expressed the pleasure he had experienced. The Royal party then went towards the river,

underneath the beautiful cedars, and on a lovely slope the Queen handed her parasol to the Marchioness of Westminster and planted an oak, which she took from the hand of Lord Warwick. Prince Albert at a suitable distance planted a "Wellingtonia". The Royal party, after the planting had been performed, returned to the Castle.'

Her Majesty's subjects who either owned or visited country houses enjoyed a way of life that was regarded as distinctly old-fashioned less than half a century later, when Ralph Nevill published *English Country House Life* in 1925. 'The amusements of an English country-house party during the Victorian era were simple in the extreme compared to those of to-day,' he suggested. 'To begin with, the men did not see nearly as much of the ladies as is now the case, generally only joining them for a cup of tea and for an hour or two after dinner. The rest of the time (after smoking indoors had come in) was passed in the smoking-room, though, of course, the sexes met for croquet, lawn tennis, or one of the round games which were once popular.

'On summer afternoons the hostess with her lady guests would go and sit in the garden, there to while away the time with a little needle or fancy work. Occasionally someone would read aloud, the arrival of the latest three-volume novel from London being something of an event. Drives to neighbours' houses were of course indulged in, but before the days of motors the radius was naturally limited, and people saw little of one another if they lived farther away than nine miles. Garden parties of a much more formal and stilted kind than those of the present day were events looked forward to for weeks beforehand by young people who were not then satisfied with the amusements so easily to be obtained by those of the present day. Life indeed was full of mild excitements which would not now attract the slightest notice. When, for instance, the guests at a country house party had

been marshalled previous to going into dinner, all the maids of the household would gather together in excited groups, out of sight, at the top of the staircase, in order to feast their eyes upon their masters and mistresses making a solemn procession to the dining-room.'

For all this languid ease and formal display, the practicalities of staying in many historic houses in the nineteenth century left a lot to be desired; in winter many were bitterly cold and any guest wanting a hot bath to warm up would have searched in vain. When the Duke of Wellington entertained Queen Victoria at Walmer Castle in 1842, Lady Lyttleton was one of the party and described the occasion none too fondly in a letter to a friend. The castle, she observed, was 'a big round tower, with odd additions stuck on. Immense thick walls and a heap of comical rooms of the odd shapes necessary as parts of a round house, built close on the shingly beach … It seems needless to go out for air, doors and windows all chatter and sing at once, and hardly keep out the dark storm of wind and rain which is howling round … All this outward rudeness

mixed very oddly with the numbers of smart servants and courtly whispers and very tolerably got-up imitation of the palace mummeries we have contrived indoors.'

'Though a few of the larger mid-Victorian country mansions had one bathroom,' writes Ralph Nevill, 'such conveniences were non-existent in smaller country houses, the owners of which were inclined to look upon such things as innovations of an unnecessary kind. When such modern sanitary appliances were becoming fashionable a visitor from town said to a squire, "Why don't you have bathrooms put in your house?" "I don't see the use," was the latter's reply. "After all one can always have a bath in one's bedroom – if one wants one!"'

The cold and damp of many great houses was exacerbated in the eighteenth century by the widespread practice of washing down walls before a party. A century later, little had improved and, shivering in the great hall of his Northamptonshire home at Deene, the Earl of Cardigan was moved to complain to his butler about the excessive chill.

'You must eat your hair, my Lord,' the butler replied.

'What, what, eat my hair?' replied Lord Cardigan.

'Yes,' the butler answered, politely but firmly. 'You must eat your hair.'

When his employer finally registered what he was suggesting, a heating system was commissioned, making Deene one of the earliest houses of its kind to benefit from the improvement.

For many families, of course, life on their country estates was balanced by life in London during the social season, and in the eighteenth century many great houses remained largely unoccupied since their owners preferred town life to country life. On the other hand there were others who, having no pace of their own to pass the months away from London, were obliged to lead a peripatetic existence moving from one house to another, living off the hospitality and good nature of friends and relatives.

According to Ralph Nevill, 'Those who owned country estates made a regular migration once a year, after the season, the whole household being transported with much fuss and bustle. Once installed in its rural abode no further move was made till the end of the next spring when the whole caravan once more made its progress back to London. As for those people who had no country house of their own, those who were able to do so made elaborate arrangements to spend as much of their time as they could in a round of long visits to friends or relations in various parts of England. The round in question, when possible, lasted from immediately after the season till the beginning of the next year. In many cases, no doubt, the hosts or hostesses who received these urban migrants did not look forward to their arrival with any particular pleasure. Bethinking, themselves, however, of the old adage "What can't be cured must be endured," they regarded the advent of a certain amount of old maids and crusty old bachelors as one of the decrees of Providence which no one could set aside. In some cases, however, the arrivals from town contributed a note of life and gaiety which considerably enlivened country life.'

Country houses were closed up for extensive periods for reasons other than a preference for town life. Sir George Sitwell, great-grandfather of the twentieth-century literary trio Edith, Osbert and Sacheverell Sitwell and owner of Renishaw Hall in Derbyshire, was one of several nineteenth-century owners of historic houses whose outgoings always outstripped their income. In 1846 this disparity finally caught up with him through a combination of events. In addition to the expense of his style of living, his finances were crippled by a catastrophic fall in land values and the collapse of the Sheffield Land Bank, which folded the day after Sir George had deposited many thousands of pounds realised through land sales. To makes matters worse, the brother of the Sitwell family solicitor absconded with £34,500 of their money. For two years Renishaw was shut up while Sir George and his wife and family were obliged to take an extended tour of small German towns, where the cost of living was significantly cheaper.

Two generations later, his eccentric grandson (also christened George), drew up imaginative plans to reshape the Renishaw gardens and wider estate, showing that only three years before the outbreak of the First World War that would change the world he knew for ever, there were still members of the landed gentry contemplating estate changes on the scale of that with which 'Capability' Brown had inspired their eighteenth-century ancestors.

'Now all the wild schemes which have accumulated for fifteen years are to be carried out,' wrote the young sub-agent at Renishaw Hall in 1911, commenting on Sir George's plans, which could at last be funded from the sale of a valuable picture by Perugino to the American financier Pierpont Morgan. 'White, the landscape gardener was here several days last week and Lutyens one day. Already we are moving the entrance to the Chesterfield Approach a hundred yards towards Thirby Cliff. A drive to Foxton Wood is planned which will cut up no end of good arable fields and entirely re-arrange the fences and plantations. Three lakes are to be made in the Eckington Woods Valley. A new drive is to be made through Cadman Wood. A new drive and terrace are to be made through Twelveacre Plantation and Goodness knows what is to be done to entertain a crowd of people in the field between the woods when Osbert comes of age. The drive is to be continued to the Ford past Never Fear Dam. The Ince Piece Wood is to be reconstructed. A swimming-bath is to be made under the waterfall, and the waterfall raised to three times its present height. A crowsfoot vista is to be cut in the Wilderness, for which plans have had to be made and platforms erected to be able to see where they would strike. Terraces are all to be pegged out. A pavilion is to be made in the lake. (Lutyens' idea is a stone ship). An extension is to be made at the top end of the lake, ditto near the Sawmill, and the Sawmill is to be moved, etc. etc. etc. What next, I wonder? . . . He is talking quite seriously about this lot. Heaven help us if he does a tithe of it. I find no time for anything except taking levels. Estate work will be in a pretty mess presently.' (Sir George's son, Osbert Sitwell, subsequently commented laconically of his father's grand schemes, 'In the end, owing to various circumstances, nothing happened at all.')

We can only surmise what those 'various circumstances' might have been. The shortage of manual labour after the First World War, which brought about the dramatic reduction in domestic servants in historic houses as well as garden staff to maintain the elaborate Edwardian grounds that surrounded them, would surely have been one. The Wall Street Crash of 1929 had repercussions in financial markets round the world and few aristocratic families escaped without some diminution in the value of their assets. Then there was the global recession of the 1930s. Taken together, they presented an insurmountable obstacle to the ambitions of a man even as single-minded as Sir George Sitwell. In these global economic setbacks lay the beginnings of the steady decline that afflicted many historic houses throughout the first half of the twentieth century.

The predicament in which many found themselves in the late 1930s was only exacerbated by the six years of privation brought about by the Second World War. Even the most celebrated historic houses were brought into

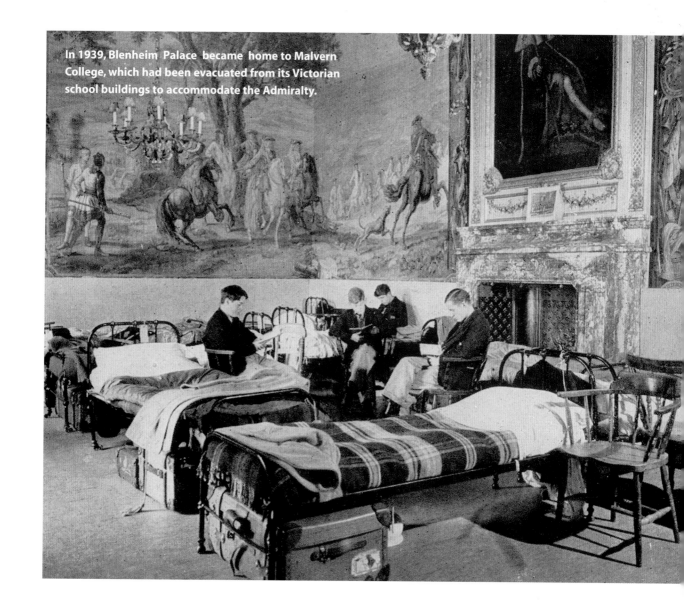

In 1939, Blenheim Palace became home to Malvern College, which had been evacuated from its Victorian school buildings to accommodate the Admiralty.

During the Second World War up to twenty girls from Penrhos College used the State Drawing Room at Chatsworth as their dormitory after the school had been evacuated from its own site in North Wales. Many other rooms in the house were commandeered for the benefit of the schoolgirls.

service to aid the war effort, with many, including Chatsworth and Blenheim, providing war-time accommodation for boarding schools which had been obliged to evacuate their own premises for the duration.

Even after the Second World War, when a new generation of owners struggled to preserve their ancestral homes, they had to contend with the shortages and rationing of the post-war years. So it was less than forty years ago that the economic climate favoured the wider creation of new business ventures designed to earn enough steady income to maintain historic houses and their estates and, most importantly, to undertake the huge task of making good the repairs and restorations to buildings, their décor and collections that had been impractical for fifty years or more.

For most historic houses the success of their business ventures rested on developing the commercial potential of their houses and estates, shifting the principal focus of their income-producing activities from a traditional agricultural economic base to a service industry concentrated on tourism and high-revenue hospitality. But bluntly, it meant opening the house and grounds to the public and offering a range of attractions and facilities which could compete for the expenditure visitors and clients had at their disposal.

Such undertakings marked a radical change in the home life of many owners. Some, of course, had had an early taste of what it entailed since many houses had taken to opening their doors to visitors for a few days a week back in the 1950s or 1960s. Even so, when the numbers of visitors and the days that houses were open to the public increased, normal daily life for the families living in them had to make significant adjustments.

Lady Diana Ingilby was one of many of her generation who continued to live in their historic houses after responsibility for them had passed to their offspring. When Ripley Castle had been constructed in the Middle Ages, the builders had not been asked to take into consideration parties of visitors being guided through it. When alterations were made in later centuries, the only concern had been for the immediate household:

the Ingilby family and their servants, plus the occasional guests.

Even a generation ago, Ripley Castle, like the majority of historic houses in private ownership, was still primarily a family home. Sir Thomas Ingilby fills in the background: 'Whereas previously my parents and grandparents had been able to use the whole house – because it was only open one day a week, so they could use the rooms on the other six and a half days – that became impossible once opening increased from

The Ingilby family photographed in the Tower Room at Ripley when it was still a family home and only open to visitors on Sunday afternoons.

Saturdays and Sundays, to four days a week, to daily during the summer months. So, we could only really occupy the rooms on the public tour on a very occasional basis and occasionally in the evenings, or on Christmas Day and times like that.'

Was that something the family resented?

His answer is measured and pragmatic. 'I don't think it was. By that stage my sisters had left home, so we weren't a large family and we weren't exactly pressurised for space. We were quite happy to retreat to a corner of the Castle. Although, until Emma and I moved in, the landing upstairs, where my mother lived, was actually an open archway with just a rope across. So she remembers well gong into her bedroom to wash her hair and then having to time her dash to the remainder of the flat when there wasn't a party coming. Of course, frequently she would be unlucky and would emerge from her bedroom with her hair wringing wet and then the door of the Tower Room opposite would open, and this party would be greeted by the sight of the dripping dowager. It was Emma and I who decided that we couldn't continue to live like that. We created a greater degree of privacy for ourselves, but we still haven't entirely solved it.'

And what about their children? The Ingilbys have five – how do they cope with their home being visited and used by large numbers of people?

'They've always grown up with it,' their father says. 'It's remarkable. For years we've operated with marquees outside the Castle with bands and discotheques playing until two o'clock in the morning, literally within thirty yards of their bedroom windows, and they have just slept right through it. That's what they're used to. It's like living in London, you don't notice the aeroplanes any more, or the underground. It's just there.'

Although, as Sir Thomas admits, it was difficult for his mother to adjust to the increasing number of visitors to the Castle. Well before his father died she had been running a café for visitors in the old outdoor servants dining-room. There she made sandwiches and served cups of tea to the twenty or so customers that could be accommodated at any one time.

69

Lord and Lady Devon and their family at
Powderham Castle enjoying a special occasion
which is also now available to the paying public.

That arrangement suited the number of visitors to the Castle thirty-five to forty years ago, as did the trestle table under the gate house where they bought their entrance tickets and possibly some garden produce that might have been laid out for sale as well. It's a far cry from the smart computerised admission suite that greets visitors to Ripley today.

There was a similar change round of family accommodation at Powderham Castle in the early 1990s, when the present Earl and Countess of Devon took up residence. 'We raised our family in the stables house down the drive,' Lady Devon explains, 'and Hugh's parents lived here and then we swapped over in about 1990. We moved up to the Castle, by which time our family had gone really, and Hugh's parents, in their old age, lived down there.

'What happened was that Hugh's parents opened the Castle to the public in 1957 and they moved upstairs into a beautiful flat up on the first floor. When we moved into the Castle we found it really silly living upstairs when you're living in the country. You wanted to let the dog out and you

had to go down in the lift, so we thought we'd move back down to the ground floor, where we live up and down a staircase in part of the house that isn't open to the public …

'In the evening, come five-thirty, it's our turn to enjoy the place. At times it does get a bit overwhelming, but with people who are interested it's just a joy to have them here.'

Like many owners, Lord and Lady Devon have got used to having to lead their lives outside their own living quarters very much in the public eye during the daytime. 'Outside our little back door into the yard [where their cars are parked] is where everybody gathers. So when you see a strong man you can ask, "Would you mind giving me a hand with the shopping?"

The physical process of creating a modern home inside a castle that dates from the Middle Ages is not without its challenges, as Lady Devon recalls: 'In order to live here, we needed to alter a few rooms upstairs, to put bathrooms next to bedrooms. I can't tell you what a mess the place was before: there were two staircases running

71

Today's house 'guests' at Ballindalloch Castle enjoy the same comforts and hospitality that friends and family would have done in days gone by.

parallel. But you couldn't move from one staircase to the other without going down to the bottom of the Castle and walking across to it. What we wanted to do was to make the one staircase, which was obviously the servants' staircase, into bathrooms, so that from each bedroom you could have a bathroom. It meant knocking through a very thick medieval wall and also opening up the other enclosed staircase to make some landings.' Logical as the proposal was, the actual implementation took eighteen months before work could begin.

Installing bathrooms at Ballindalloch Castle in Banffshire was a less tortuous procedure because each of the bedrooms had been provided with a closet large enough to accommodate a bathroom. So the friends and house parties who stay in the Castle throughout the year are able to enjoy a level of period elegance and personal comfort unmatched by any five-star hotel.

Ballindalloch receives around 18,000 visitors a year and with the layout of the castle restricting large groups from being given a guided tour together, people are free to make their own way through the public rooms. This relatively low-key arrangement makes it possible for the Lady Laird and her family to make use of all the rooms all the time. 'Bedrooms that we use to accommodate guests the whole time are quite often off the tour,' says Mrs Macpherson-Grant Russell. 'Having thought that people would be cross seeing a notice saying "Terribly sorry, the family have friends staying", people love it because they feel that it's being lived in. If we have lunch in the dining-room, if we've got a lot of people, visitors love nothing more than opening the doors after we've finished and seeing things being cleared away, because they can actually see that it's lived in. People love hearing what's been on the menu. It's fun.'

Occasionally the realities of coping with sixteenth-century defensive architecture can prove too much for a visitor and at times like this it is very helpful to have the Laird or another member of the family around, who is able to step in and lend a hand. The Highland Tower at Ballindalloch dates from the mid-1540s and was built with a narrow stone stairway, which changes direction halfway up, before rising to the Watch Tower. This proved to be the undoing of one visitor who, as Mrs Macpherson-Grant Russell describes it, 'was a wonderful lady who got part of the way up the tower and couldn't go up or come own, and was totally frozen to the spot. She and I had to go down on our bottoms on this very cold stairway all the way to the bottom, because she wasn't going to get down any other way.'

Although this might be an extreme example of the kind of difficulties than can arise when trying to open to the public an old Highland castle with narrow passages and cramped access, Mr and Mrs Russell are deeply indebted to the expert help on arranging the dynamics of opening a house to large numbers of visitors they received from Norman Hudson. 'It was essential when we opened up to the public to have his guidance,' Oliver Russell confirms. 'How to organise the movement of people. How people actually arrive in the house. It's very important how you actually circulate people and Norman Hudson was very helpful.'

The Russells were also fortunate that Ballindalloch Castle has wings, which made it easier for them to live in their private quarters at one end, without having to have too much of an upheaval in order to accommodate daily visitors. James Hervey-Bathurst says the same about Eastnor Castle, where his family have always lived in the south end. 'It has smaller rooms and was always designed for family,' he adds.

Eastnor had been opened to visitors on occasions in the past. In the 1950s and 1960s, the principal rooms in the Castle were more sparsely furnished than they are today, but visitors' level of expectation was less forty or fifty years ago. James also makes the significant point that the families who owned houses of the size of Eastnor Castle never had them entirely to themselves: 'Historic houses have always had people in them. If you were brought up in an any sizeable house, even in London, there were always staff about … The difference now is that the people who are working here are not focused on our needs, they're focused on the needs of the business and the customers of the business.'

The sparse interior of the Great Hall at Eastnor as it once looked.

In days gone by children brought up in historic houses, often by nannies, experienced a level of privacy that many of their modern counterparts have never known.

Melding these modern needs with maintaining a degree of privacy, especially for growing children, requires careful handling. 'Part of the visitor attraction is that there's a family living here. So it's a difficult balance,' he admits.

In some houses, the owners move out for the summer. 'And that may be the pattern in the future,' James acknowledges. 'If the house is big enough as a business and my daughter chooses to live in another house, she could come here to work and use it occasionally, as we do now, to entertain her friends on a grand scale.'

'It would be a pity,' he accepts. 'We could easily run this house but not live in it. I could come to the office in the normal way and be available all day to deal with issues … But I'd prefer to be here. The other side is that my children regard this as home and it's always sad for children to have to leave home.'

It's sad too when a family has to sell their ancestral home. As president of the Historic Houses Association James Hervey-Bathurst knows more than most about the challenges and contemporary realities of living in and running a historic house. 'People are proud,' he tells you. 'Selling is tantamount to failure and nobody wants to be the one who has broken the long line of family tradition … You always meet people who regret that their family house was sold, maybe by an earlier generation, but of course it's quite difficult for them to project forward to what their life might have been like had the house survived and they had to look after it.

'Generally it's a privilege still living in a house like this. It's constantly interesting. You meet interesting people who come through because they want to look at something that you're doing, or at part of

The Gothic Drawing Room – the popular perception of aristocratic privilege.

77

your collection. But it's a qualified privilege. It comes with hard work and lack of privacy.'

There is no denying the remarkable turnaround in their fortunes that houses like his have undergone as a result of inspired and dedicated investment of time, energy and limited financial resources. However, speaking as a professional with considerable experience of working in the heritage business in both charitable and privately-run properties, Stuart Gill from Newby Hall in North Yorkshire sounds a note of caution: 'There's a very interesting debate on the way that historic houses have developed … There's a real roundabout scenario that you attract more visitors, therefore you spend the extra money on catering for those visitors and you go round and round and round. More visitors, therefore you need a bigger car park, more marketing, more staff to look after them.

'We did that exercise when I was first here. We stood back and asked, "Why do we open the gates?" There are lots of reasons, but one of the main driving forces for me is to try to generate enough income to keep the gardens and the

house on an upward curve of improvement, rather than just being static or slightly downhill. So there's a big challenge when we sit round at the AGM and decide, with the wind in the right direction, that we might make £10,000. Should we reinvest that in restoring one of the pictures? Or should we refurbish the paddling pool? That's a real debate that we have.'

'It's a very important debate,' agrees Richard Compton, for whom Stuart works as administrator. 'Because the *raison d'être* of opening the house to the public is to maintain it for the future. Lucinda, my wife, is a furniture restorer and she sees the condition of some of the furniture, which has never been able to have huge amounts of money spent on it, because there have always been extra demands because of the increased public requirements. She comes forward and says, "That piece of furniture has got to be restored, otherwise it will collapse." And it means it will take X-amount of money etc., etc. It's very important to get the balance.'

Here, Richard Compton gets to the core of what it means for many historic house owners to be 'living over the shop' – to live surrounded by collections of incredible beauty and value, housed in a lovingly created environment of exquisite craftsmanship – and having to juggle the work of what amounts to being a fine art curator-cum-clerk of works with that of the managing director of a five-star hospitality business-cum-family entertainment venue. And all of this has to be achieved largely through the successful running of the business: for, as a privately-run non-charitable venture, publicly funded grants for Newby Hall and similarly managed historic houses can often prove to be limited.

He quotes an example to reinforce the point, which many owners in his position will recognise. 'We sat

The new entrance pavilion at Newby – an expensive but necessary investment in visitor facilities.

down at the AGM three years ago [in 2003], after our best year ever and discussed what we wanted to do with the tiny bit of profit. We discussed restoration of a piece. We discussed extra work in the garden, putting in a borehole for the watering system – all of those sorts of things. In the end we had to build a new loo block in the car park, which cost £35,000. It's one hundred per cent geared towards the visitors. It's never used in the winter.

'We also had to build a new entrance pavilion, because the one that my father built twenty-five years ago was a combination entrance and shop, which was fine for 80,000 people a year. But when you've got 150,000 people, the only thing you can do is build a new entrance pavilion for £200,000. That's empty in the winter as well.'

'These are the sort of clashes that you've got,' Richard Compton concludes. The irony is, that if his parents had not been successful in their running of Newby Hall as a business, and if other historic house owners had not built and sustained equally successful businesses of their own, they would all have been forced down a different

heritage route – one that would have qualified them for the kinds of grants they are rendered ineligible for by virtue of managing to keep going and grow their own businesses without recourse to large-scale external support.

The last word on this topic should rightly go to James Hervey-Bathurst, who speaks for many owners of historic houses when he makes the point that, 'Glossy magazines obviously talk up the luxury, the wealth of art and, by implication, the privilege of houses. That's fine, up to a point, because that is what they are all about and always were all about. But what we're talking about nowadays is qualified privilege and the fact that most houses that are in a good state and moving forward are used in a different way, and are places where things have definitely changed.

'Yes – there are marvellous houses with works of art and families still living in them as they have for many years, but they're living in them in a very different way from how they used to, and perhaps how many people think they do.'

Living History

One of the great attractions of visiting historic houses is, self-evidently, their link with the past. This can be achieved in a variety of ways, but the most tangible and readily accessible is through the architecture of the house itself, through its internal décor and the collection of art and artefacts, gathered over the centuries, that reflect the taste, style and way of life of previous generations.

In some instances rooms we see today, even whole houses in a few cases, have been inspired by particular historic events, which lends them an immediacy that visitors latch onto. Loseley Park, for example, was built by Sir William More, a favourite adviser to Queen Elizabeth I, who evidently wished to stay at his home except for the fact that the old medieval house 'was not mete for her to tarry at'.

Sir William's descendant, Major James More-Molyneux, explains that Sir William was not a wealthy man, 'but he took the hint and built a House that was "mete" to receive the Queen'. It took him four years and cost £1,640 19s 7d. 'The building of Loseley House was a great work,' writes Major More-Molyneux, 'and one hopes that it gave Sir William real satisfaction. Queen Elizabeth did come and stay with him in his House on four occasions; she must have appreciated the efforts that her friend had made in building the House for her convenience, but the Queen was a demanding guest. One letter gives instructions for the drive to be strewn with straw to avoid the jolting of the carriage, and that the House should be cleaner than on the last occasion. The Queen brought a considerable retinue with her and Sir William's family and staff were required to move

Loseley – the house 'commissioned' by Elizabeth I so that she could visit its owner Sir William More.

Queen Elizabeth's room, still with some of its original furnishings and textiles.

into the medieval house which still stood on the South Lawn.'

'In 1968, to celebrate Loseley's 400th birthday,' Major More-Molyneux's account continues, 'we had an evening's excursion back to an earlier era, with an Elizabethan Banquet attended by 140 guests in the Great Hall, most of them in Elizabethan costume …

'We all felt the wonderful atmosphere that evening. The scene in the Great Hall was stunning in the candlelight; music and song came from minstrels in the Gallery. The House was enjoying its birthday evening. The Elizabethan costumes were so decorative, the rich colours of the velvet tunics and beeches contrasting with the few dinner jackets and black ties. The food was ample and delicious [and authentically Elizabethan]. The mead, honey based and known as the honeymoon drink, was deceptively alcoholic.

'Yes, life in Elizabethan times was good,' Major More-Molyneux reflected, 'if you were wealthy, if you were on the right side of the right religious denomination and if you escaped the rack and the axe and if you did not have appendicitis or toothache, or married without father's consent.'

The guided tour of Loseley House includes a close-up of those times in a visit to Queen Elizabeth's Room, where the hand-made bed and window curtains and the carved oak pelmet are the original ones that Sir William More's royal visitor would have known when she stayed there.

Either side of the hearth of The Drawing Room at Loseley are a pair of Elizabethan Maid of Honour chairs with cushions, which are believed to have been worked by Queen Elizabeth herself. This handsome room retains a memento of another royal visit, this time made by Queen Elizabeth's successor, King James I. The magnificent gilded ceiling was decorated in his honour.

King James I is remembered in a ceiling at Ripley Castle where The Tower Room was the principal bedroom in the early 1600s. On his way to his coronation in London in 1603, the king sent a message to Ripley that he would like to spend the night of 16 April in the Castle. In a frenzy of activity and no doubt with an eye on future royal favour,

The gilded ceiling of the Drawing Room at Loseley was designed to honour a visit by James I.

the Ingilbys busied themselves making ready for the visit and went as far as rushing in the plastering team to put up a new ceiling at breakneck speed in the king's honour. The fruitfulness of his reign was symbolised by pomegranates and sweetcorn on the beams. Royal symbols denoted the presence of royalty and the family emblems of a star and boar's head were prominent to indicate the family's loyalty to their new sovereign.

History does not relate what King James thought of these gestures, but the involvement of members of the Ingilby family in the Gunpowder Plot two years later can't have helped their attempts to win his approval. (In spite of this, a generation later the Ingilbys were staunch supporters of King Charles I, and the resolute Trooper Jane Ingilby even held Oliver Cromwell at pistol point in the library at Ripley on the night of his crushing defeat of the Royalist army at Marston Moor; while she did this her brother, William, lay hidden in a secret hiding place in the Knight's Chamber at the top of the Tower.)

A further perspective on history can be gained from the pictures, sculpture, porcelain and furniture

The Statue Gallery at Newby Hall containing examples of sculpture collected by members of the family undertaking the Grand Tour.

that give each house its special feel. The very nature of such collections provides an interesting commentary on the way that earlier members of the family spent their time and their money. The Grand Tour, which completed the education of aristocratic gentlemen in the eighteenth century, provided an obvious conduit for works of art acquired during visits to the Continent.

However, amassing a fine art collection was not without its temptations, or perils, as the celebrated Earl of Bristol and Bishop of Derry was to discover. He succeeded to the family estate at Ickworth near Bury St Edmunds in 1779 and became known as one of the most enthusiastic collectors of art of the age. Travelling abroad for many years, he spent freely and frequently found himself short of money as his passion for enhancing his collection regularly emptied his purse. At one particularly awkward stage, he wrote, 'All my effects at Rome are under sequestration to the amount of £20,000 at the very least. All that immense, valuable and beautiful property of large mosaic pavement, sumptuous chimney-pieces for my new house,

and pictures, statues, busts and marbles without end, first-rate Titians and Raphaels, dear Guidos and three old Caraccis – *gran Dio*! *Che tesoro!*'

His contemporary commentator, Lord Cloncurry, recorded in his memoirs that the Earl-Bishop 'received £5,000 a quarter which he immediately expended in the purchase of every article of vertu that came within his reach. In this, as in most other cases, however, the proverb came true – wilful waste made woeful want; and towards the end of the quarter the noble prelate used to find his purse absolutely empty and his credit so low as to be insufficient to procure him a bottle of Orvieto. Then followed the dispersion of his collection, as rapidly as it was gathered but, as might be expected, at a heavy discount.'

The legendary eccentricities and excesses of William Beckford, who inherited so a vast a fortune that he became the richest private citizen in Britain, built one of the largest houses of his day and amassed one of the finest art collections held in private hands, contrast with the more sober approach to establishing ancestral homes and family collections adopted by his contemporaries.

Born into a wealthy family in 1759 William was indulged in a manner his mother considered appropriate. He had Mozart for a music teacher (the musical prodigy was, himself, only a child at the time), and was introduced to such luminaries as the French philosopher Voltaire. Surrounded by all the splendour of the family home the young squire of Fonthill grew up with every advantage but little rein on his petulance or 'unbridled temper'.

When a scandalous relationship with William Courtenay, third Viscount Courtenay of Powderham Castle, forced him abroad, Beckford fled to Europe where he spent the next thirteen years as an itinerant, moving from the home of one European noble to another. On his eventual return to England he threw himself into the business of embellishing Fonthill in a lavish manner. Still blacklisted by society, he chose to surround the 519-acre estate with a twelve-foot-high wall and began the business of building the most remarkable folly of a home that England has ever seen.

Beckford's inspiration came from Salisbury Cathedral, yet Fonthill Abbey, as it was officially called, is perhaps the most famous building disaster of all time. James Wyatt, who had just completed the delightful Music Room at Powderham, was employed as the architect, and hundreds of men were taken on to undertake the job. Beckford insisted they should work on a shift system so that building could continue twenty-four hours a day and as encouragement he plied the men with drink. The combination of exhausted and inebriated workmen, shoddy

craftsmanship, shabby materials, an unsuitable design and Beckford's impatience did little to ensure that the structure would be long-lasting. The three hundred-foot octagonal tower at the heart of Fonthill fell down three times before it finally stayed put long enough for Beckford to believe it was secure.

At the same time William set about creating the right surroundings for his 'Castle of Atlas', as he called the Abbey, and the garden that he lavished his fortune on is considered to be one of the finest examples of the time of 'natural' landscaping.

When the Abbey was more or less completed in 1813, Beckford said of it, 'the Abbey cannot be contemplated without emotions that have never been excited by any building erected by any private individual in our times'. What Beckford might not have expected was for those emotions to be ones of frustration and anger.

Certainly the Abbey was large enough to house the enormous collection of art, furniture and objets d'art that Beckford had built up over the years. His library contained 20,000 volumes in his own binding. He adorned the walls at Fonthill with paintings by Canaletto, Raphael, Rembrandt, Rubens, Titian and Velasquez, among others; and twenty of the works that Beckford once owned are now in the National Gallery. He also owned magnificent collections of Venetian glass, and a table from the Borghese Palace at the centre of which lay the largest onyx in the world. Beckford amassed the world's largest collection of Japanese lacquer work, including the superb 'Van Diemen' black lacquer box which is now in the Victoria and Albert Museum, where many of his other treasures are housed.

How well this magnificent collection fared at Fonthill is debatable. The chimneys smoked, the wind whistled through the windows, the roof leaked and the state of the tower foundations threatened its imminent collapse. Several years later when Beckford's financial affairs took a decided turn for the worse, he sold Fonthill for £300,030 and moved to Bath. In time the grandest folly in England collapsed taking Beckford's grandiose dreams with it.

Of course, not all visitors to historic houses felt qualified to appreciate the collections to their full; some even felt intimidated by them and sought other diversions. In 1841 Sarah Spencer, Lady Lyttleton, accompanied Queen Victoria on a visit to Woburn Abbey and found the experience very staid. 'How dull!' she wrote. 'Bless me! We are eleven of us, Dukes and Duchesses, and most dukefully dull indeed we are. The Queen must carry away with her a strange idea of what society and conversation mean. The material is all very fine. That is, the place is handsome, the house most comfortable and huge, and the dinner also, after a great and unconcealable effort contrives to be *almost* as sumptuous as our daily fare at Windsor … the Queen seems always afraid of asking questions about pictures and portraits for fear of being thought ignorant, so the part of the business she liked best was peeping into everybody's own rooms.'

On visits to Chatsworth Queen Victoria would have been shown the treasures of that great collection, though accounts of her time there do not indicate whether she felt the same inhibitions when confronted with works of art that Lady Lyttleton had detected at Woburn. Helping visitors to understand better what they see in the state rooms at Chatsworth has been important to the present Duke and Duchess of Devonshire, who have undertaken a degree of reorganisation in these famous rooms.

'They were done in a very traditional Chatsworth way of accumulation,' the Duke explains, 'an archaeological delight with different generations of stuff arriving from different places … It is a perfectly acceptable and good intellectual approach to a house, because it's the way that one's own home builds up. You buy something when you're thirty and if it doesn't break it's still there when you're sixty; but it's not contemporary with the rest of the house.

THE KING'S VISIT TO THE DUKE OF DEVONSHIRE: THE ROYAL PROCESSION PASSING THROUGH CHATSWORTH GATES.

VISIT OF

THEIR MAJESTIES THE KING & QUEEN

TO

CHATSWORTH.

ADMIT BEARER TO ROWSLEY STATION,

Monday, January 4th, 1904.

JOHN MATHIESON,

GENERAL MANAGER.

'However, I didn't really understand the state rooms and if I didn't understand them, nobody except for a few people here [at Chatsworth] would understand. So we set about making them a bit more like the way they would have been when they were first built.'

So the changes were made and, as the Duke acknowledges, 'That caused quite a lot of people quite a problem to start with, particularly the Great Chamber which looks very empty, because it is very empty … One or two letters came saying that it was a great pity. And one or two people made it quite clear that while they respected our right to change it, they thought it was a mistake. That's fine. I don't have a problem with that at all. But I do think that it's a significant improvement. I think it's much more interesting and I think it's much more dramatic.'

'Interesting' and 'dramatic' are words that were certainly applicable to 'Beyond Limits', a selling exhibition of modern and contemporary sculpture mounted by Sotheby's throughout Chatsworth's magnificent gardens over seven weeks in the early autumn of 2006. 'The quality of the art in it shines out,' wrote the art critic Richard Dorment. 'and its placement around the park is as witty as it is surprising, thanks to the eye of guest curator Janice Blackburn.'

Although not part of the Chatsworth collection as such, 'Beyond Limits' highlighted the link that has always existed between works of art, the house and its glorious setting. The present Duke and Duchess have a strong interest in contemporary sculpture and some of the pieces they have collected are on display in the house and garden for visitors to see and enjoy.

'Ever since the first Duke, there has been contemporary, or old sculpture, put in the garden here,' the Duke explains. 'Most of the main collectors who have spent time at Chatsworth have put sculpture in the gardens, in the same way that they put paintings on the walls.'

'The advantages [to the Sotheby's show] are severalfold,' he continues. 'There is a fee. There is our own interest, which is perhaps the least important. And I think the most important part is that it will attract people who either haven't been

here for a long time, local people who feel they know it very well, or people who haven't been to Chatsworth because they feel it's an old house with lots of old stuff in it …' [This applied particularly to educational parties, with 400 teachers planning to bring 5,000 students to see this inspired display.]

'We're doing it because it's an interesting way to use these amazing spaces that we have for something different,' says the Duke. 'It's exactly the same as putting on the Country Fair. It's using an available space for something which is interesting and rewarding for people, which some people will like more than others.'

Since the majority of pieces Sotheby's had placed in the sale are designed to be displayed out of doors, they could be shown to advantage in the gardens at Chatsworth. This was clearly the reaction of Richard Dorment, who said of one striking example of the interplay between sculpture and setting, 'There isn't a bigger cliché in art than Robert Indiana's bright red sculpture spelling out the word "LOVE". Yet, seen from a distance in the middle of the dramatic cascade, it looks sensational, one of the few art works I can think of visually powerful enough to register against that man-made cataract without distracting our attention from its beauty.'

For the Duke of Devonshire, the Sotheby's show was a very interesting landmark in the development of Chatsworth and the way people view it. As he puts it, 'There are lots of things that happen here that are always the same, principally the landscape … The inside of the house, the visitor route has changed significantly and will change more, but most of the objects are the same. So it's very nice to have something that is really very different from what went before, to come for a short period and then go away again.'

In the field of painting, the collection at Ballindalloch Castle has a similar feel of historic continuity about it. This came about, as Mrs Macpherson-Grant Russell explains, somewhat by chance: 'My father, before he died, said that there were some ghastly pictures in the attic and he'd been told by a professor that they were bonfire material. He said that we ought to get Sotheby's or Christie's just to look at them before they were put on the bonfire. Anyway we had Sotheby's and Christie's, and they suddenly became the largest collection of seventeenth-century Spanish paintings in private hands in Scotland!

'Having said that, they're all fairly deep, dark and depressing. But Sir John Macpherson-Grant in 1850 had collected all these Spanish paintings and they are in fact of great interest to Scotland and the family.'

The present-day Spanish connection was inspired by the late Lord Nicholas Gordon-Lennox, who had been British Ambassador in Madrid. It was he who asked Mr and Mrs Russell if they had done anything about commemorating the Millennium, specifically having a portrait painted of the family. He explained that he had come across a young Spanish painter during the course of his work in Madrid and thought that he might be suitable.

'We looked at his style,' Oliver Russell says. 'We liked his style. It was the first one he had ever done of a group of five and so, from that point of view we got in relatively early, which made it affordable and there we are.'

The artist who painted the laird and her family is Paco Carvajal and his portrait of them hangs at one end of the delightful dining room at Ballindalloch. Equally pleasing from the family's point of view, and for the history of the Castle, is the portrait of General James Grant by Allan Ramsay that also hangs in the dining room. The general had been presented by George III and Queen Charlotte with paintings of them both (also by Ramsay), in recognition of his military

service in the American War of Independence. These royal portraits also hang in the dining room and, in Mrs Macpherson-Grant Russell's opinion, 'I think that picture [of the general] has gone back to where it originally was, because the marks of the picture that hung there match that picture exactly – and the light also. I think it must have been sold, and anyway we found it in Christie's and bought it last year.'

Sir Brooke Boothby is among other historic house owners who have enjoyed the same kind of satisfaction from the restoration of items that had been lost to the collection. 'There was a silver gilt cup from 1678 that was lost for a hundred years,' he explains, referring to an extraordinary piece of good luck at Fonmon Castle. 'It was found in a box in a London solicitor's and when that solicitor's closed down in 1911, they cleared their offices and found this box with it in. And we'd never have had it otherwise, because one of us went bust in the meantime, so he would have sold it for sure. That, as a child, had always appealed to me – that something could lie in a dusty office for a hundred years, from about 1817 to 1911. It was given as a gift by the wife of the second baronet to him as a twenty-first wedding present.'

Among acquisitions and additions he has made himself, Sir Brooke has bought a second edition Bishop Morgan Bible, because the Fonmon library had never had an old Welsh Bible. 'So, when my godfather died,' he says, 'they decided to sell his library to pay their death duties. And I bought it in from Philips's at auction.'

Other owners have been able to use profits from businesses established to maintain their historic houses to undertake equally satisfying purchases to enhance their collections. After a comprehensive refurbishment and redecoration programme that brought much of Eastnor Castle back to its former glory, thereby making it feasible to accommodate paying house parties, James Hervey-Bathurst saw that some additional furniture and fittings were required. 'After we'd got as much furniture out of storage as we could,' he begins, 'we found we needed a few things for the walls. I bought four tapestries and a Gothic sideboard, lots of smaller things: 100 lamps and lighting units around the

place, because there weren't enough lights. Nothing spectacular, except that I did buy back a portrait of my great- great-great-grandmother, which was sold in 1904. It's not a great a painting. It's a modest addition to the collection, but it's nice to bring it back here. And it's small additions like these that make the house a much nicer place to visit.'

After plenty of years of things going out of their houses, it's a source of great satisfaction to owners who can start to bring them back in again. At Ripley Castle, Sir Thomas Ingilby says, 'We've started to buy the odd painting and a bit of furniture, and we're gradually restoring the collection … It's very pleasing to be able to do that, particularly restoring works of art that have been allowed to run down over the years.'

In doing this, of course, historic houses are helping to support and maintain a wide range of craftsmanship, perpetuating skills in restoring and maintaining paintings and furniture that might otherwise struggle to find full employment. There can surely be no more rewarding and productive way of keeping history alive.

Sporting Scenes
and Film Locations

Historic houses have provided the setting for all manner of entertainment since the days when hunting parties of medieval aristocrats rode the countryside and ancient woodlands in pursuit of deer, boar and anything else that took their fancy, while inside the great halls of their castles they passed the evenings dancing or enjoying the performances of itinerant musicians. Elements of this survive in country house life today, although the number and range of guests has been extended enormously by the creation of commercial shoots on many great estates, coupled with the provision for paying house parties of fine dining and sumptuous accommodation in the house itself – an innovation that has only come about within the last thirty years. At the same time the setting, atmosphere and décor of historic houses make them sought-after locations for film and television production companies.

Although leasing sporting rights and running formerly private shoots as commercial enterprises is commonplace today, it is not a recent phenomenon. Writing as long ago as 1925, Ralph Nevill noted that the practice was by no means uncommon and indeed had been in place for fifty years or more. 'One of the greatest changes indeed in the mental standpoint of landowners is the way in which they regard the letting of their estates for sporting purposes,' he observed. 'As late as the middle of the last century the aristocracy and gentry did not at all approve of

allowing strangers to pay for the right of shooting over their estates, the letting of grouse moors and deer forests which was then just beginning to come in, being considered as a vulgar and plutocratic innovation by the old school, which openly expressed its disgust at those squires who, to fill their pockets, let their shootings to city men somewhat apt, it was said, to shoot keepers and generally outrage the usages traditional among sportsmen. The shootings of those days were, as a rule, very poor compared with those of to-day, cockney sportsmen, as they were called, being comparatively easily satisfied, and never thinking of demanding the luxurious accommodation which is considered essential to-day. As a rule, the neighbouring squires and their wives left such people severely alone, deploring the incursion of urban barbarians into the country-side, and vowing that they themselves would always keep their shooting in their own hands. Since then, however, mainly owing to stern necessity, these squires have found themselves obliged to place their estates in the agents' hands, and as early as the seventies and eighties the letting and

selling of country houses and of sporting rights had come to be considered quite a reputable manner of increasing a landed proprietor's capital or income.'

Until well into the nineteenth century, though, county house entertainment followed a pattern that would have been familiar to generations of earlier owners and guests. Hunting was a popular pastime, which in some cases amounted to an obsession. George, Earl of Orford, was an eighteenth-century 'sportsman' notorious for his extravagances. Ralph Nevill commented of him, 'His mania for driving stags one day nearly caused him to be torn to pieces by a pack of hounds he chanced to encounter upon the Newmarket Road. Fortunately he had the presence of mind to put his strange four-in-hand into a gallop, and eventually managed to steer it into the yard of the Ram Inn, now the Rutland Arms, just ahead of the pursuing pack. A great patron of sport, this Lord Orford eventually met his death through taking a dive from a window. A coursing match was going on close by, and eager to see it, he seems to have been in too great a hurry to adopt the conventional method of going out by the door, with the result that he fell on his head and died.'

William Henry Vane, who succeeded his father as third Earl of Darlington, was cast in a similar mould as a Regency man of 'the chase'. 'Most of his time was spent as a sportsman,' commented the author of *English Country House Life*, 'rather than as a great noble or a politician, at his Durham castle of Raby.

'A great sportsman, Benjamin Marshal painted his portrait on horseback with his hounds, which painting was engraved by J. Dean in 1810, and published by W.D. Jones, Cambridge. He is represented wearing a cap, but at a later period he abandoned this for a tall hat, and made his hunt servants do the same, considering it to be a better protection. Lord Darlington hunted his own hounds for thirty-eight years; his country, it may

be added, is now [in the 1920s] hunted by the Zetland, the Bedale and the Badsworth hunts, an enormous tract of land according to modern hunting ideas.'

Two figures prominent in the sporting set of the Victorian era were Sir Frederick Johnstone and Sir George Chetwynd, who, according to the author of *English Country House Life*, 'were sportsmen pure and simple. Without their stables and their race meeting they would have had no occupation, though both had figured in well-known passages of English social history. Sir Frederick Johnstone had won and lost heavily; Sir George Chetwynd, while on the whole not unsuccessful with his horses, owing to the huge expense connected with a racing stable, died anything but a rich man. Both were pleasure-seekers of the type to be seen at fashionable resorts like Monte Carlo, not necessarily playing high, but always enjoying life in a well-bred way.'

Of all country-house pursuits, shooting is probably the most widely followed these days, although it is far less of a hit and miss activity than it was in its early days when guns were muzzle-loaded and birds flew away from the sportsmen pursuing them, rather than being driven towards them. Here is Ralph Nevill again, on shooting as it used to be: 'Before the days of the breech-loader it was customary for the host at a shooting party to provide powder and shot for his guests. This, of course, was not such a serious item as providing cartridges, and when the latter came into fashion the old custom naturally lapsed. Before battue [driven-game] shooting had become a regular feature of country-house life the bags made were usually comparatively small. Guns did not shoot so straight or shooters aim so well as has since been the case … A case in point was Lord Palmerston who, when he missed, would sometimes lay the blame on the wind somewhat after the style of the foreigner who complained that the English rabbits were too short. During his later years, Lord Palmerston, then as fond as ever of the sport, was known to fire off both barrels at birds a hundred yards off; indeed, as long as he could get his gun off he was usually quite satisfied even when there could be no result. It was told of another noble lord (Lord Ashbrook), who never touched a feather during an entire day's shooting at Holkham, that the keeper, by way of consolation, remarked that he had seen people shoot worse than his lordship. "How can that be, when I missed bird after bird?"

"'Aye, but your lordship misses them so clean.'"

While the shooting season provided male guests and their hosts with excellent outdoor sport, the winter hours during which they were absent often hung heavily for the ladies left behind indoors. The Countess of Warwick had the questionable good fortune of being married to one of the best shots in England. As a consequence she and her husband received invitations to the grandest and most coveted shoots, where the Earl displayed his marksmanship and the Countess her tolerance of days of perpetual boredom. 'We began the day by breakfasting at ten o'clock,' she wrote. 'This meal consisted of many courses in silver dishes on the side-table. There was enough food to last a group of well-regulated digestions a whole day. The men went out shooting after breakfast and then came

A shooting party at Blenheim with Queen Victoria's eldest son,
the Prince of Wales, understandably taking centre stage.

the emptiness of the long morning, from which I suffered silently. I can remember the groups of women sitting discussing their neighbours or writing letters at impossible little ornamental tables. I never could write at spindly-legged tables … We were not all women. There were a few unsporting men asked – "Darlings." These men of witty and amusing conversation were always asked as extras everywhere to help entertain the women; otherwise we would have been left high and dry. The ladies rarely took part in the shoot … We changed clothes four times a day. This kept our maids and ourselves extraordinarily busy. When I think of all these gorgeous gowns round a tea-table I fancy we must have looked like a group of enormous dolls. Conversation at tea was slumberous. Nobody woke up to be witty until dinner-time with its accompanying good wines. The men discussed the bags of the day and the women did the admiring.'

Queen Victoria's eldest son and his wife were regular winter visitors to Chatsworth, both as Prince and Princess of Wales and, from 1901 following the death of his mother, as King Edward VII and Queen Alexandra. The king was a keen shot and with Chatsworth offering some of the finest shooting in the country, the Duke of Devonshire's royal house parties at the turn of the twentieth century attracted a great deal of interest. The night-time drive from Rowsley station, four miles from Chatsworth, was described by one commentator as being 'rendered very picturesque by the flickering light from the hundreds of torches of the linkmen, who lined the route for nearly a mile. The house itself was floodlit by arc lights and, despite the winter cold, large crowds gathered at the gates to cheer the King and Queen. The account in the illustrated weekly newspaper, *The Graphic*, of their visit in early January 1904, gives a detailed picture of an Edwardian royal house party familiar in many great houses of the time.

'The programme arranged for the Majesties' stay at Chatsworth as the guests of the Duke of Devonshire was largely provisional, and the weather prevailing during the later hours of Monday night did not augur well for a day's sport in the Bunker's Hill Hare Park and Birch Hill coverts. Luckily, however, the fog had lifted, and though there was sufficient haze to render distant objects dim, the conditions were not sufficiently adverse to prevent the guns going out to the well-stocked coverts. In expectation of the departure of the sportsmen a crowd gathered at the north end of Chatsworth House, and here and there, people collected on the grassy slopes through which the main avenues branch.

'Overnight the King and Queen and Princess Victoria had been present at an impromptu dance which followed dinner. Yesterday morning the carriages for the shooting party were ordered for half-past eleven, and within a quarter of an hour the departure was made. Two brakes with postillions were used. The King was in the first brake, and with him were six gentlemen of the house party. The Duke of Devonshire drove the second, and was accompanied by other guests. His Majesty wore a fur cloak, and his headdress was a Homburg hat with a feather …

'The destination of the party was a point high up on the hillside beyond a square turreted structure called the Hunting Tower. Shooting was brisk,

pheasants falling rapidly. There are open sheets of water in the vicinity, and wild duck also fell to the guns. A hundred beaters were out, and birds were brought down so fast that a large game cart was speedily loaded.

'Arrangements had been made for lunch in a marquee near a keeper's lodge known as the Swiss Cottage, and here the sportsmen were joined by Queen Alexandra, Princess Victoria, the Duchess, and ladies of the house party. A few elected to climb the steep on foot, but the intention of the Royal ladies to drive became generally known, and as the luncheon hour approached there was a second gathering of the public. The first open carriage to emerge from the

grand entrance contained the Countess of Gosford and Lady Alice Stanley; and a moment or two later an open wagonette in which was Queen Alexandra passed out …

'After luncheon shooting resumed. The King rode to more distant coverts on horseback, accompanied by Lord Howe, who was mounted on a Basuto pony. The Marquis de Soveral accompanied the Queen to Chatsworth, her Majesty returning by way of the grand cascade.

'The shoot, which had been followed very closely by a number of the Duke's tenants, came to an

Gamekeepers at Powderham then and now.

end at about half-past three o'clock. The King and Duke walked back the private way, to the disappointment of the crowd gathered round the main entrance to Chatsworth House.

'A number of members of the house party, among whom was Mr Balfour [prime minister at that time], went on to the golf course, and played during the forenoon and part of the afternoon. With them were Mr Ben Sayers and Mr Taylor, the well-known professionals. Mr Balfour played Mr Evan Charteris and won. Other players were the Ladies Acheson and Mr Sidney Greville. The course is delightfully situated, having at one extremity a famous relic – a low, square-walled enclosure surrounded by a moat, and called Queen Mary's Bower, from its having been a favourite place of resort with that ill-fated Queen of Scotland during her sojourn at Chatsworth.

'The Princess Victoria and the Duchess of Devonshire availed themselves of the comparatively favourable weather to drive through Bakewell, where the natural features are swelling uplands and rich meadows and sparkling streams. The arrival of the Princess and Duchess in the neighbourhood was not generally known, but one or two motor cars followed the route out and back to Edensor.'

The crowds of onlookers may have been disappointed not to see His Majesty walking back to Chatsworth that afternoon, but royal visits afforded plenty of opportunities to see the royal visitors. On another occasion, seven years earlier, the then Princess of Wales and other ladies had joined the shooting party for lunch resulting in 'a great outburst of cheers and waving of handkerchiefs, which the Princess graciously acknowledged'.

After lunch 'The guns were posted at the most likely spots on the Edensor paddocks, and here one of the best possible pheasant drives took place. Birds were plentiful, and as they fell rapidly at the feet of the sportsmen increased excitement took place in the crowd which had assembled to witness the sport. The bag must have been a very heavy one, numbering at a rough estimate some 500 or 600 brace [1,000–1,200] of pheasants as well as other game, rabbits, &c.'

While daily bags of that size are unusual now, primarily because of the costs involved (most days' shooting being priced by the number of birds shot), the volume of shooting on many estates is probably greater than it has ever been. This requires careful management, though successful commercial shoots can account for a significant share of estate income, and income in the wider rural community, as Sir Thomas Ingilby makes clear in his book *Yorkshire's Great Houses*: 'Most estates derive vital income from leasing or syndicating their shooting rights, and this sport now plays a vital role in the rural economy during the otherwise quiet time between November and the end of January. If they have travelled from another part of the country, the party is likely to spend one or two nights at a local hotel, spending more money on restaurant food and drinks at the bar. If the guns are local, they will buy their cartridges, kit and clothing from local suppliers and a typical shooting day might provide employment for two gamekeepers, a dozen beaters, a tractor driver and a couple of pickers-up retrieving any dead or wounded game that falls behind the line. The party may go to a local pub for lunch, or the gamekeeper's wife or some other helper may prepare and serve it in a luncheon hut on the estate, a local village hall or in one of the houses on the estate. They are keeping a lot of rural people in work at a time when employment in the agricultural sector has shrunk by over twenty per cent in the last decade.'

Like many busy owners of historic houses, Sir Thomas leases the sporting rights on his estate at Ripley to a tenant, who organises all the shooting, employs the gamekeepers and supplies the vehicles. 'He runs the shoot to a far more professional and better level than I could ever hope to.'

109

Part of the reason for this is that Sir Thomas's tenant is running together several adjoining shoots, to increase the acreage under his control. This enables him to offer clients about 110 days shooting a year, thereby generating significant turnover for his business. 'It's a very nice arrangement,' Sir Thomas agrees, 'and we were incredibly lucky in the gentleman we got to run the shoot … He does do the job well and he really loves the challenge of running a good shoot. It's not just a numbers game for him; he wants it to become one of the best shoots in Yorkshire.'

Ripley benefits in more ways than receiving rent from the running of a successful shoot. 'A lot of the guns will stay in the Boar's Head [which is owned by the estate, with Sir Thomas as licensee]. Some of the shoot lunches are here. Some of the beaters will go back to the Boar's Head for a meal afterwards. Some of the smarter parties will take a dinner in the Castle the night before to entertain their guests. So the shoot is a very important part of our business.'

James Hervey-Bathurst is of the same mind, agreeing that shooting is 'a very good winter business' on his estate in Herefordshire. 'We have a private syndicate that shoots the outlying woods and drives,' he explains. 'Then we have a commercial shoot for the main part. The guests mostly stay in the house; so it gives us a good stream of business in the house in the winter.'

Eastnor Castle is fortunate in lying only ten minutes from the national motorway network and two and a half hours by car from central London, which makes it easily accessible to clients from all over the UK and those flying in to Birmingham airport or those around London. When your castle lies 500 miles further north in the glorious, but relatively remote, countryside of the Spey valley in Banffshire, you have to look to developing a different kind of hospitality business.

This was the challenge that faced Clare Macpherson-Grant Russell and her husband Oliver, when they took over the running of the Ballindalloch Castle estate in 1978, though they would admit that the business they have developed came about almost by chance when a group of Oliver's fellow bankers asked if they could combine a scheduled series of meetings with some field sports. This was barely a couple of weeks after the Russells had taken up residence. In the words of Ballindalloch's Lady Laird, 'That started our corporate entertaining, which really saved the whole estate.'

'There's a fundamental background that has totally changed,' her husband continues. 'In the days of Clare's father, and indeed prior to that, the rent from a let farm would enable you to employ several people. It changed, so that now you need a number of farms to pay one person. That is the fundamental change on Highland estates, which

In the nineteenth century the Ballindalloch estate employed many more agricultural workers than it is able to do today.

means that you've got to work a lot harder and choose other things in order to employ people. You would never maintain an estate with the level of farming there is now.'

The day-to-day running of the Ballindalloch estate is now in the hands of a factor, who is kept well occupied. 'We did up seven houses,' Mrs Macpherson-Grant Russell says. 'Two or three are fully staffed and they house our fishers. We have twenty-four rods per day and we house all of those fishermen, which brings in quite a lot of money. Of course, in the old days, my parents didn't commercialise anything, because you didn't.'

Ballindalloch offers a full range of Highland sporting facilities, of course: shooting and stalking, as well as fishing, and now golf. Its glorious setting and the opportunity to stay in the house that is widely acclaimed to be 'the castle everyone would love to live in', means that Mr and Mrs Russell have opened their doors to a fascinating mix of visitors. 'We have enjoyed every minute of our house parties,' Mrs Macpherson-Grant Russell writes in the introduction to her mouth-watering recipe book *"I Love Food"*, 'and our lives have been enriched by our guests. We have entertained chief executives, Ambassadors, Prime Ministers, Royalty and Hollywood Stars over the years and have made many delightful friends worldwide. Looking back over our twenty-five years, we would not have changed the way that we have welcomed the house parties. They have given us great joy and the Castle never feels happier than when it is filled to the brim with people.'

In the woods which lie to the back of Fonmon Castle in the Vale of Glamorgan a different kind of shooting reflects a popular pursuit in the country houses of days gone by: archery. In this case, however, Sir Brooke Boothby makes no charge for the Welsh National Field Archery competiton course laid out there, because its presence has been a great help in the Castle's security: 'Beware Arrows' is a very effective sign for discouraging unwanted 'visitors' from entering the castle grounds. At no cost to the estate, security around Fonmon Castle has been vastly improved and Welsh archery has benefited as well.

On one occasion in the summer of 2006, another sporting event brought two of Fonmon's varied activities into rather too close proximity, but that only serves to point up the balancing act that many historic houses have to maintain when they may have more than one function taking place on the estate at the same time. An email from Sir Brooke Boothby relates what happened: 'This w/e entertainment was a couple who said, "We want nothing to do with the World Cup. No televisions, no radios. We will arrive at 5 pm. Party for 160 guests starts at 5:30."

'By 3:55 there were over eighty guests present, all expecting to watch the match – no hosts, bar not open, florists still working. By 4:10 we had four screens running and the bar open, and by the time the hosts appeared over 140 people were happily cheering and groaning.

'Unfortunately the general noise had attracted the attention of some followers of the UK Field Archery Championships which were going on in the woods surrounding the house, so when the hosts arrived they found several people happily ensconced who were nothing to do with them. Luckily everyone was very good-natured.'

The Boothby family was heavily involved with hunting during the last century, in fact from the earliest days of hunting as we know it. Sir Brooke's grandfather was Master of the Vale of Glamorgan Hunt, his great-great-uncle was Master, and so was Sir Brooke's mother. 'My mother actually hunted them [the pack of hounds] for ten seasons as things got tougher and tighter. Rather than having a professional huntsman, she hunted them herself, which was quite sporting. Except for one day when she got on her horse and fell straight off it because she had such bad flu. She simply couldn't sit upright. She was very tough, mum; a very serious hunting lady.'

However, even Lady Boothby must have been more than a little taken aback by an exchange with a very grand English lady whom she met at a

Lady Boothby (mother of Sir Brooke) with the Vale of Glamorgan Hunt with which the family had close connections for several generations.

114

house party for the first time. Knowing nothing of each other, they sought to establish a shared interest and she was asked, 'Do you hunt?'

'Yes,' Lady Boothby replied.

'Very good … and which pack?'

'I'm with the Vale of Glamorgan,' Lady Boothby answered.

Her answer clearly flummoxed the other house guest, who enquired, 'Where's that?'

'In Wales,' she was told.

In answer came a reply out of centuries back. 'Good Lord. I didn't know one hunted in Wales.'

There was nothing rude intended in this remark, it was simply beyond her comprehension that a lady would hunt in Wales, quite overlooking that the Vale of Glamorgan Hunt was approaching a hundred years old and indeed had held its centenary dinner in Fonmon Castle.

'I don't think my mother ever spoke to her again,' says Sir Brooke. 'They were her pack and she was hunting them, but I don't think she ever mentioned that. There again, the other lady would have been equally scandalised that a woman should hunt her own pack.'

Today, that close connection has parted. 'It's very sad,' Sir Brooke confesses. 'The Boothbys in particular were absolutely in on the founding of hunting. If you go to Leicestershire, Thomas Boothby of Tooley Park founded the Quorn [Hunt] in 1696 – he was almost the founder of hunting. There's been a big involvement for generations, so it's slightly sad that it's gone.'

Sir Brooke's mother was the last member of the family able to devote herself to the sport. The present generation have too many other demands on their time, he explains. 'For instance, I never learned to ski because we were inevitably hunting flat out all through the Christmas holidays and the early part of the Easter holidays … So, you didn't ski if you were a true hunting family. The very grand ones did because they shot off in mid-April, to somewhere high up and went

skiing. But average hunting families never skied. Now, the kids are just not here.

'That also changes the staffing question,' Sir Brooke points out. 'Because of course there was a stud groom, two under-grooms. Now, there is no one in the stable at all. There are still the horses, but they belong to children of the staff.'

The growing up of the Courtenay children brought similar equestrian changes to Powderham Castle, near Exeter. When the current Earl of Devon and his sister, Lady Katherine Watney, were growing up and active in local pony clubs and gymkhanas, their parents started the Powderham Horse Trials, which ran for nearly forty years. 'We took on the running of it,' says the present Countess of Devon, 'and it became one of the longest established horse trials in the country. But when we decided to give it up, because our children had stopped competing and our daughter was getting married ["and because it's jolly hard work", interjects her sister-in-law], and we thought we'd done it long enough – honestly the flack we got! "You can't not run Powderham Horse Trials, it's just not on." We were made to feel

very much as if we'd let the side down by not running it.'

The Powderham estate certainly provides a wonderful setting for horse trials and riding here clearly appealed to Hollywood star Christopher Reeve and his wife Dana, when he spent a fortnight at Powderham filming the Merchant-Ivory production, *The Remains of the Day*. 'Christopher Reeve became a great mate,' says the Countess of Devon, who rode regularly with the actor and his wife around the Powderham event course during his time away from the cameras.

The Remains of the Day, based on the remarkable Booker Prize-winning novel by Katzuo Ishiguro, tracks the gentle decline of a great English country house from the 1930s into the post-war era, through the eyes of its long-serving butler, played in the film by Anthony Hopkins. In tone and tempo it mirrors *The Shooting Party*, adapted from the novel by Isabel Colegate eight years earlier in 1985, and described as a 'Merchant-Ivory lookalike'. This too takes as its central theme the decline of aristocratic country house life and the society it epitomised, set here in the last shooting season before the outbreak of the First World War in 1914. While both these films counterpoint the end of this kind of exclusive and private country house hospitality in their respective eras, they represent for the current owners of Powderham Castle and Knebworth House (where *The Shooting Party* was largely filmed) – and every similar property used as a period location – another lucrative means of turning the attributes of their houses and estates to their advantage. And just as

with the letting of shooting rights as far back as the end of the nineteenth century, there is nothing new in historic houses providing background settings for film and television productions.

In the mid-1920s one commentator bemoaning the loss of a number of mansions in the hard years after the First World War gave a graphic example of what could lie in store in the more extreme examples of film collaboration. 'A short time ago,' he wrote, 'it was announced in the Press that the characteristic old Georgian mansion of Sudbrooke Holme, about five miles from Lincoln, was likely to be purchased by a British Film Company, who proposed to burn it to the ground in order to produce a spectacular scene on the cinematograph.

'The mansion in question has for several generations been associated with the Sibthorp family and is one of the noted county seats of Lincolnshire, for which reason strong local feeling was aroused, with the happy result that Sudbrooke Holme has been acquired for public purposes by the Lincoln Corporation. The utilization of old country houses for film purposes of a less destructive kind will probably become more usual as time goes on, historic seats forming an ideal setting for realistic scenes connected with a past age.'

Ninety years after that observation was made, the use of historic houses by film and television production companies provides their owners with another, albeit occasional and fairly disruptive, source of income.

In the case of Powderham Castle it was ease of use and the freedom to cause an inevitable degree of disruption that encouraged Merchant-Ivory to ask if they could film there. The sensational Staircase Hall was a major attraction for them, as was the splendid canopied bed in the State Bedroom, which formed the centrepiece of Lord Darlington's bedroom; even though he (played by James Fox) slept on a camp bed at the foot of it.

Lord and Lady Devon were able to remain relatively undisturbed in their private part of the house, leaving the film crew to get on with what

they needed to do in the public rooms. They used to be invited to watch the rushes in the evening, which made them feel part of the process and the cast evidently formed a close attachment to Powderham and the people there.

'Anthony Hopkins was absolutely great,' Lady Devon recalls. 'He was slightly aloof during it all, but at the end he drove away in his chauffeur-driven car and was half-way to Exeter when he suddenly asked his driver to turn round because he had forgotten something and needed to go back to Powderham. So he arrived at the front door and asked "Where's Peggy?" – the wonderful old lady who used to clean here, who'd been here for ever.

'Peggy was duly found, busily cleaning away. "Peggy, thank you so much for looking after us so well. It's been absolutely wonderful being at Powderham," Anthony Hopkins told her. Peggy was completely bowled over. He gave her a photograph of himself, which he signed. Gave her a peck on the cheek, which she never washed off! He was so kind – so appreciative. A good man.'

In some instances providing the setting for a costume drama, particularly a television series, can increase visitor numbers dramatically. 'The big productions pay reasonable location fees,' writes Sir Thomas Ingilby, 'but if the programme is a success, the real benefit can come from the publicity and profile associated with it. The spin-offs from *Brideshead* [*Revisited*] kept Castle Howard busy for more than a decade, and made it a household name in America, where the programme was an even bigger success than here.'

Sir Thomas has first-hand experience of the visitor-pulling power of television after Ripley Castle was chosen to be the location for the filming of the children's drama *The Flaxton Boys*, which ran for four series from 1969 until 1973. 'That put Ripley well and truly on the map,' he says.

'I'll never forget the Easter Bank holiday after the series had first been on. They'd forgotten to put a credit for Ripley on some of the episodes, so they said, "I'll tell you what, we'll give you some TV advertising instead." And my father said, "That's

very kind of you," not realising what was about to happen. Suddenly that Easter Bank Holiday over 1,000 people descended on the castle every day and the system just couldn't cope. We didn't have anything like the facilities to handle that number of people. It was absolute chaos. My mother said you could almost see the mortar squeezing out of the walls, there were so many people inside the Castle.

'The knock-on effect was that the numbers just continued, not quite on that early level. But we were getting hundreds a day, not just twenty. So we always knew that we had to improve those facilities to cater for those people.'

Something very similar happened to Eastnor Castle, when the BBC filmed a screen adaptation of Frances Hodgson Burnett's children's novel, *Little Lord Fauntleroy*, at James Hervey-Bathurst's family home in 1994. Simon Foster, who is now the general manager of the Castle and Deer Park, has good reason to remember that production: he was the BBC's location manager working on it and it literally changed his life. 'It was the spring of 1994,' says Simon. 'We lived in London, had just

started a family and [moving to Eastnor] sounded like a nice career change.

'My involvement with the production lasted about twelve weeks. The first four of that was finding locations and setting it up. Then eight weeks of filming, followed by the post-production process before it was broadcast … I was with the project for about three months and we filmed at Eastnor for four of those eight weeks.'

Simon's brief had been 'to find a large, imposing late-Georgian or early-Victorian house that reflected the status of Lord Dorincourt who's the central character in *Little Lord Fauntleroy*. It was a difficult location to find in a sense, because *Hudson's* and all those other books document these properties very well. Once we'd found our central location at Eastnor, we found our satellite locations within a ten or twenty-mile radius. That was my last BBC job and I swiftly moved from that into this job.'

His timing couldn't have been better: 'It was a rather nice start for me. It was broadcast in the early part of 1995 and we then opened to the public at Easter and the visitor numbers went from 15,000 to about 40,000 in one year. It was a huge jump.'

With the income from a day's filming amounting to the income from one wedding, it's understandable that historic houses are prepared to put up with a fair degree of inconvenience caused by a week or more of filming, when it makes a contribution of that order to the bottom line of the balance sheet.

'There's obviously more upheaval with a film,' explains Michael More-Molyneux, 'but if you can get a week's filming that means you've got seven days of weddings, which is fantastic.'

His home, Loseley Park in Surrey, is easily reached from London, which makes it a sought-after location for a pretty wide variety of productions. 'We had a big-screen production, *Amazing Grace*, which is all about Wilberforce – that was a week's filming. For three weeks we had *Foyle's War*. Ten years ago the Spice Girls movie was filmed here. We had *Spook*. Last weekend [in the summer of 2006] we had a day's filming for *Jane Eyre*. Miss

Marple came three times last year [2005]. It's all good revenue.'

Asked how disruptive filming in the house can be, Michael replies laconically, 'You don't want to decide to have a dinner party for twenty friends. It is very intrusive. They always want to do things and move things – all the time … But you accept that and you realise that you have to babysit them and it's much better that way. Sarah and I make sure that we walk through, so that they know we are around.'

Throughout September 2006 Newby Hall in North Yorkshire was taken over by a film company making a television adaptation of Jane Austen's novel *Mansfield Park*, starring Billie Piper. Welcome as the income is, Richard Compton indicates that it's not without its challenges: 'We've got one or two weddings coming up in the month, or corporate events. We've got the Darlington Dog Show going on, which is 15,000 dogs and their owners. It's all happening. Then we've got a craft fair coming up.'

His administrator, Stuart Gill, also explains that this is the biggest single filming project that Newby

Newby Hall 'cast' as Jane Austen's Mansfield Park in a TV adaptation filmed in 2006.

has ever undertaken. 'The filming is a one-off, as well as a cash injection,' he goes on to say, 'but also there's also a considerable value to it in PR terms.'

'It will be good promotion and it could be a boost for us next year,' Richard Compton adds. Before filming began, considerable thought was given to how its impact on the house could be kept to the minimum, bearing in mind that no visitors could be admitted to the house for a whole month while the cast and crew were working. 'Part of the contractual negotiations has been that they will be using one room and when they have finished there, we can actually move our own furniture back comfortably, slowly, using our own people,' Richard says. 'With any luck, in a month's time we'll be able to look back and say it hasn't been as bad as we thought it might be.'

Despite the best efforts of production controllers and sympathetic house owners and staff, the real world can occasionally make unscripted interventions as happened at Stockeld Park near Wetherby, during the filming of an episode of *Emmerdale*.

The house, owned by Peter Grant, often doubled as Lady Tara's manor house in the popular TV soap so, as Sir Thomas Ingilby recounts, 'the family had become reasonably used to chaos over the years, but even so, nothing could have prepared them for the fateful day when Peter's Uncle George died …

'The problem was: how to get the body out of the house? The staircase and entrance hall were crowded with milling actors and crew, so it was decided to try and remove him in a body bag via a side entrance. The bearers got halfway across the terrace outside when a furious production assistant flagged them down: "What the Hell's that body doing here? That doesn't feature in the script until next week – get it out of sight!" The poor girl was absolutely mortified when the situation was explained, and Uncle George was allowed to continue his journey to the undertakers without further interruption. Uncle George loved the absurd, and would have laughed uproariously.'